Spirit Junkie

SPIRIT JUNKIE

A Radical Road to
Self-Love and Miracles

Gabrielle Bernstein

HAY HOUSE

Australia • Canada • Hong Kong • India
South Africa • United Kingdom • United States

Published in the United States by Harmony Books,
an imprint of the Crown Publishing Group, a division of Random House,
Inc., New York. www.crownpublishing.com

First published and distributed in the United Kingdom by:
Hay House UK Ltd, 292B Kensal Rd, London W10 5BE. Tel.: (44) 20
8962 1230; Fax: (44) 20 8962 1239. www.hayhouse.co.uk

Published and distributed in Australia by:
Hay House Australia Ltd, 18/36 Ralph St, Alexandria NSW 2015. Tel.:
(61) 2 9669 4299; Fax: (61) 2 9669 4144.
www.hayhouse.com.au

Published and distributed in the Republic of South Africa by:
Hay House SA (Pty), Ltd, PO Box 990, Witkoppen 2068. Tel./Fax: (27) 11
467 8904. www.hayhouse.co.za

Published and distributed in India by:
Hay House Publishers India, Muskaan Complex, Plot No.3, B-2, Vasant
Kunj, New Delhi – 110 070. Tel.: (91) 11 4176 1620; Fax: (91) 11 4176
1630. www.hayhouse.co.in

Text design by Ellen Cipriano • Text photographs courtesy of Sam Bassett
Jacket design by Jennifer O'Connor • Jacket photography by Sam Bassett
Graffiti art courtesy of 5Pointz Aerosol Center, Inc.

A catalogue record for this book is available from the British Library.

ISBN 978-1-84850-713-5

Printed and bound in Great Britain by TJ International, Padstow, Cornwall.

MIX
Paper from
responsible sources
FSC® C013056

*For my mother. Thank you for being
my spiritual running buddy.*

Contents

PART 1 The Detour into Fear

Contents

PART 2 The Answer

PART 3 The Miracle

Foreword

Gabrielle Bernstein is both a teacher and a storyteller, looking to the truth she's found in her own everyday experiences to mine the gold that is her gift to others. She realized years ago—as I once did myself—that if there were a force that could turn her messy life around, then she'd be compelled to share her story.

Spirit Junkie teaches clearly and entertainingly how to apply spiritual principles to practical concerns, by demonstrating how Gabrielle has done so herself. From love to career to other issues involved in simply being alive in these times, you can see her trip, fall, and come right back up. Then you see her get to the point where she doesn't even fall anymore. And, ultimately, you realize that you've learned so much from her that you think you can get there, too. A miracle for her has become a miracle for you.

Gabrielle has reminded me of our first encounter. Years ago, having stood in line to speak to me after one of my lectures, she asked how I would apply the principles of *A Course in Miracles* to people her age. To that I responded, "Read and study the *Course*. Then ask God how you should share it with your generation." I figured that that was her job.

I was right. And she has done it well.

This book is the story of Gabrielle's personal journey, but it is a story that instructs us all. Her sincerity, her willingness, and her true humility before the teachings of *A Course in Miracles* give her the requisite power of a genuine teacher. May her teaching grow, flourish, and deepen with the years. She has clearly been assigned a most beautiful task, helping legions of people move beyond their psychological and emotional darkness to a spiritual light that she herself has seen. With *Spirit Junkie*, she continues her work. Thereby, may she and all her readers be blessed.

—*Marianne Williamson*

Spirit Junkie

Introduction

The journey that we undertake together is the
exchange of dark for light, of ignorance for
understanding. Nothing you understand is
fearful. It is only in darkness and in ignorance
that you perceive the frightening, and shrink
away from it to further darkness. And yet it is
only the hidden that can terrify, not for what it
is, but for its hiddenness.

—A COURSE IN MIRACLES

• ◆ •

For more than twenty years I kept a journal. In it I wrote about heartbreak, anxiety, and eating disorders. I wrote about trying to quit drugs while high on drugs. Pages and pages are filled with self-loathing, self-doubt, and a running calorie count. I wrote the same romantic mini-drama with dozens of different names attached. My journal entries were my only outlets from the turmoil and deep-rooted pain I lived with every hour of every day. Through writing I'd release my fears onto the page and get honest about my sadness as I scribbled over my tears.

Today my journal entries are much different. They reflect an empowered woman who is happy and bleeds authenticity. Instead of dwelling on my diet or obsessing over romance, I use my journal to honor myself. The words on the page are tinged with pride and compassion. I've overcome my addictions to love, drugs, food, work, fear—you name it, and I've recovered. I worked hard, and man, was it worth it. Today each of my journal entries shows a deep desire to continue growing from the inside out.

My primary guide on my journey to self-love has been

the metaphysical text *A Course in Miracles*. The *Course* is a self-study curriculum emphasizing practical applications for relinquishing fear in all areas of life. The *Course*'s unique thought system uses forgiveness as the road to inner peace and as a guide to happiness. I was first introduced to the principles of the *Course* through the spiritual teacher Marianne Williamson, known throughout the world for her best-selling books and her international speaking circuit. Marianne is the leading teacher of *A Course in Miracles* and is a straight-up spiritual rock star.

The *Course*'s lessons have taught me to view my life and how I experienced it in a totally new way. I've learned that much of what I feared in my life was not frightening at all, or in many instances even real. I've learned that fear is simply an illusion based on past experiences that we project into the present and onto the future. For instance, I came to realize that my experience of being dumped by my high school boyfriend had morphed into an illusion that I held on to for more than a decade. This simple adolescent breakup managed to morph into a belief system of unworthiness and debilitating fear of being alone.

The lessons of the *Course* allowed me to see how I replayed this fear from the past in all my relationships from high school onward. In every new relationship I began, I'd drag the baggage of that breakup in with me. Even as I was basking in the happiness of being with someone I liked, in the back of my mind lurked a constant fear that my happiness could be snatched away at any moment, and I'd be faced with the same heartbreak and trauma I'd experienced in that high school relationship. Ultimately that fear would cause me to sabotage my new relationship. When the relationship was over I'd try to anesthetize my pain with food, work, and—worst of all—drugs. I'd do whatever it took to avoid feeling my fears from the past. I was unable to savor simple pleasures and happy moments because I was constantly on guard against fear. This cycle was endless. I'm thankful that the *Course* taught me that the fear I had been lugging around for so many years wasn't even real, that it was just an illusion I had created and was projecting onto my current experiences. Once I experienced this realization, I was able to work through the fear. The more I committed to this new belief system, the less I replayed my past in the present. In time I began to release those fears and witness miraculous changes. This realization was revelatory in that I'd awakened to the fact that if I stuck to the *Course*'s plan I could truly relinquish my fearful patterns.

Admittedly, when I first began reading the *Course*, the language and many of the concepts were extremely foreign to me. Each time the text would refer to "God" or "the Holy Spirit," I'd totally freak out. But, ultimately, I came to realize that getting bogged down in semantics was a silly distraction. What mattered most was the guidance the *Course* had to offer me at a time when I needed it most. The words were just a vehicle to all the valuable lessons that were available within its pages. I learned that what really mattered was how relevant the *Course's* teachings were to my life, and my absolute willingness to be guided to change.

It was with that burning desire for change that I set out to purchase the *Course* to begin with. Upon entering my local bookstore, I noticed the sturdy-looking dark blue book with the title *A Course in Miracles* scrawled in gold lettering across the cover. Instead of being daunted by it, I found the thickness of the volume inviting and reassuring. So much so that I smiled as if I had received a wink from the Universe as I grabbed the book off the shelf. Then the most auspicious thing happened. The book literally dragged me to the counter. No joke. I physically felt the book dragging me to the register. It felt strange and yet oddly comforting. Intuitively, I knew I was in for something good. I bought the book immediately and walked out of the store. As I stood on a busy New York City streetcorner, I flipped the book open to its introduction and read, *"This is a course in miracles. It is a required course. Only the time you take is voluntary. The course does not aim at teaching the meaning of love, for that is beyond what can be taught. It does aim, however, at removing the blocks to the awareness of love's presence, which is your natural inheritance."* This passage sent chills down my spine. I'd found what I was looking for, a guide to removing all the crap that had been blocking me from inner peace and love. In that moment I made a commitment to myself to become a student and a teacher of the *Course*—a sacred contract that would change my life.

One year later, I went to hear Marianne lecture. Afterwards I had the opportunity to speak with her about my introduction to the *Course* and my desire to spread its message to my generation. I asked her for suggestions as to how I might proceed with this goal. She replied, "Read the *Text*, do the *Workbook*, and study the *Manual for Teachers*. Then get on your knees and ask God how you should share this work with your generation." I did just that.

Through reading the *Text* I was guided to understand the mission of the *Course*. Simply and succinctly, the *Course* states that *"its goal for you is happiness and peace."* The *Text* also gave me a deep understanding of the basis for my fear and guilt, and how they could be overcome. Finally, the *Text* taught me the meaning of "the miracle." The miracle is simply defined as the shift in perception from fear to love. Then I embarked on the *Workbook for Students*, which consists of 365 lessons, an exercise for each day of the year. This one-year training program began my process of transforming my own fears to love. The *Workbook* guided me to know a relationship with what I call my ~*ing*, an inner guide, or, as the *Course* calls it, an Internal Teacher. This relationship with my ~*ing* became my primary tool for restoring my mind. (I'll explain ~*ing* further in chapter 1.)

Then, when I was ready, I began to practice the *Manual for Teachers*. This section of the *Course* prepared me to share its lessons in a way that was authentic to me. As a result of my dedication to the *Course*, I was blasted open to reconnect with my true inner spirit, which is love.

My intention and my hope is that this book will act as a conduit through which I can share the beautiful, life-changing lessons that I learned as a student of the *Course*. Through the telling of my own life's stories, I will relate how the lessons of the *Course* led me to release my fears of the world and become a full-on Spirit Junkie. These days I'm addicted to finding my happiness and love inside myself. Thus the title. With this book I want to show you how to tap into your own spirit in your search for happiness. This is not a book on *how to get happiness*; rather, it's a guide to releasing the blocks to the happiness that already lives inside you. I will guide you on a journey of new perceptions and show you a whole new way to view your life. Your hangups will melt away, resentments will release, and a childlike faith in joy will be reignited.

Throughout the book I'll share personal anecdotes of how I overcame the stronghold of my ego (my fearful mind) with the help of *A Course in Miracles*. Through my *Course* work I've learned that my darkest struggles in relationships were by far my greatest teachers. To drive home this message, throughout the book I'll often refer to my parents, friends, and former lovers. (For the record, I have tons of love for these people today and am deeply thankful for the lessons I've learned from our relationships.) Through my interpretation of the *Course*'s principles you'll learn that all the safety, security, and love you're seeking is not "out there," but inside yourself. Trust me: I spent more than two decades looking for happiness in all the wrong places. I thought happiness was in a credential or a boyfriend or a new pair of shoes. I thought that if I accumulated or achieved enough, my misery, insecurity, and anxiety would somehow disappear and be replaced by joy, confidence, and lightheartedness. It never worked. Turning inward can seem like an insurmountable challenge, but by committing to the *Course* you'll learn that inward is the only place to go. When you truly know this, you can release the *need* to be saved, stop controlling, and let life flow.

I will be your teacher on this journey. Before we begin down the path, I'd like to tell you a little about myself. As a speaker, author, mentor, and coach I've made it my life's work to help others release the blocks that stand between them and their inner joy. My work has been received well throughout the world because, let's face it, who doesn't want to be happy? But let's put titles and credentials aside. The most valuable gift I have to offer you is life cred. I've lived every word in this book and transformed myself through the stories you're about to read. I once was a strung-out drug addict seeking self-worth from the outside world. Today I turn inward and receive all the happiness I'd been seeking.

The journey we're about to embark on together in this book is broken up into three parts. The first leg of the journey is Section One, "The Detour into Fear," which will explain how our minds go wrong and why we become so accustomed to fearful ways of being. Then, Section Two, "The Answer," will provide a road map to serenity. This section will give you the necessary tools for reconditioning your mind back to peace and joy. Then, in Section Three, "The Miracle," you'll be guided to maintain your happiness and share it with the world.

To help further illuminate your journey, I've created guided meditations that you can download on my site, www .gabbyb.tv/meditate. There is a meditation for each chapter. These meditations will help you reconnect with your true essence, which is love, and your birthright, which is access to miracles.

The *Course* teaches that each time we shift our perception from fear to love we create a miracle. The more miracles you add up, the more extraordinary your life will be. The outside world and all your relationships will be enhanced as a result of your inner shift. Serenity will kick in, fear will subside, and once and for all you'll know that all the love you need is inside you.

Sounds like I've got the keys to heaven, doesn't it? That's right, I do! And I can testify to these tools because I work them like a full-time job. Just breathe, be willing, and show up for the suggestions along the way. Remember you are not alone. Even if fear has you in a headlock, I'm here to remind you that happiness always wins.

PART 1

The Detour into Fear

1

A Tiny Mad Idea

All shallow roots must be uprooted, because
they are not deep enough to sustain you.

—A COURSE IN MIRACLES

• ◆ •

For most my life I felt like a fraud. I worked super hard to be perceived as cool. I did everything I could to keep up, fit in, and be accepted. I dressed a certain way, studied specific subjects, tried different hobbies. In high school I wore Doc Martens, wrapped a flannel shirt around my waist, and tried to be cute by wearing my field hockey skirt to school on game day. I did whatever I could to fit in, but none of it worked. I never felt as though I was part of the group.

I now realize that behind all my striving was a search for meaning and purpose. I was searching for a sense of self-worth in relationships ranging from friends to family to romances. My outside persona was a loquacious, white, middle-class Jewish girl growing up in the 'burbs with her divorced hippie parents. But I had no clue who I was on the inside.

To make matters worse, I felt like my thoughts were totally different from those of the average adolescent. It seemed as though my contemporaries were content to focus on sports, the latest hit movie, and dating. My mind was obsessed with other things. I constantly wondered why I was this person in this body with this family at this time. I'd think, *Is this it? We're born, we get an education, we make some money, we get hitched, we have some kids, and then we die? Is that all there is to life?* I was an adolescent girl caught in an existential crisis. My inner turmoil had me questioning everything I was trained to believe in.

The world around me taught the thinking of inequality, separateness, and competition, and better-than and less-than. I was led to value money, a romantic partner, and success as driving factors for true happiness. The world taught me to believe in archetypes like mean girls, hot guys, rich dads, poor kids, cool crowds, and losers who sat alone at lunch. I was supposed to believe this world was real, but deep down I didn't fully buy it. In my mind a battle raged between what I was taught to believe and a deep-rooted intuition that there was something more. My inner voice was screaming, *Wake up, girl, there's a better way!*

Throughout my formative years I experienced fleeting encounters with what I was seeking: a peaceful world beyond what I was taught to see. This began at age sixteen. By that time my inner turmoil had gotten so bad that I was in a constant state of anxiety. I feared just about everything. I was scared of being alone, getting too fat, not being cool enough. Some days I didn't even have a reason—I was just scared. This anxiety made me feel like a freak. My brother and friends seemed to be totally chilled-out, whereas I was in a constant state of panic. My hippie mom chose to remedy this anxiety with what she knew best: meditation. I was desperate to ease my incessant thoughts and get out of the scary world I'd created inside my mind, so I took her up on her offer to learn meditation. Once I agreed to give it a shot, my mom lit some incense and sat my ass down on a meditation pillow. She taught me to sit cross-legged with my palms facing upward so that I could receive the so-called "energy" around me. This was far outside my comfort zone, but I was distressed and willing to try anything.

Early on in my mediation practice, I confirmed that my intuition was right. There *was* a better way. I found that whenever I'd sit long enough, my mind would soften and my anxiety would disappear. Then one afternoon I was led to know much more. In the middle of my meditation I felt a rush of peace come over me. My limbs began to tingle and I felt surrounded by a sense of love. I felt at home for the first time. This experience reassured me that my intuition was spot-on. There was more to happiness than shopping malls, TV, and being popular. There was a source of energy that was greater than me, which I could access if I sat long enough in meditation. Even though I was still totally confused about my existence, this gave me something to hold on to. It gave me hope that there was indeed a better way to perceive the world.

Unfortunately, I couldn't share this experience with my high school contemporaries. I couldn't very well show up at school and say, "Hey, guys, I meditated last night and my body was taken over by a loving energy. It was totally cool." There was no way in hell they'd believe me. As far as they were concerned, *what you see is what you get.* It seemed to me that they believed in a world of separateness, fear, competition, and prom. Had I shared my existential philosophies with my friends, I'd have been exiled. I was weird enough already.

So instead I chose fear. I turned my back on the feeling of love and serenity brewing inside me and took what I thought was the path of least resistance. I detoured into fear and forgot about my encounter with love. I made the decision to go along with the crowd and believe life was tough. As I got older and grew into this mindset, I focused on the form I'd projected onto my life. I saw myself as so-and-so's girlfriend, as a theater student, as a young entrepreneur, as a party girl mentioned in the gossip rags and someone worth Googling. I portrayed myself as better than others, but on the inside I felt less than everyone. From the outside it looked as though I had successfully created a "cool" existence for myself. But I couldn't ignore the voice in the back of my mind nagging me to remember that *there was a better way.*

However, I hid from that voice. I denied its truth. I chose to let fear take the wheel and navigate my life without a road map. This choice led me to some super scary dead ends, which included a slew of addictions—drug addiction being one of them—and unhealthy, drama-filled relationships. Luckily, I got lost enough times to surrender to that inner voice, listen, and pick up the map. That map was *A Course in Miracles*, and it became my guide back home.

Today I have the map in my back pocket and I'm psyched to share it with you. I know you must be longing for a guide. Maybe you're going through a breakup, coping with a job loss, or mourning a death. Maybe you're recovering from a form of addiction, you hate your body, or, like me, you're having some kind of existential crisis. Whatever it is I know it's not easy, and that in some way or another fear's running the show. Let's face it: you wound up in the self-help section of the bookstore, right? But that's cool. Your willingness to enhance your life is what guided you to me. Where you are is totally normal. This is where most of our minds end up sooner or later. That's because, early on in life, most of us separate from love and choose fear instead. We might have fleeting moments of inspiration and truth. We feel love through a song lyric or an image or after a warm embrace. We sense love, but we don't *believe* in it. We save our faith for fear. But ultimately, there is a quiet voice in each of us that longs for something better. That voice inside *you* is what led you to this book. Some way, somehow, your inner voice of love spoke louder than fear and said, *Maybe there's a better way.* And you listened.

Nice one! I'm proud of you. You did the best you could to get to this point. So let's get the ball rolling! I'm here to guide you to a whole new way to perceive the world. As I mentioned before, A Course in Miracles will be our map. Like most maps, the Course can be hard to understand at first glance. Therefore, it's crucial that you keep an open mind. I know this New Age stuff might be a little funky for you, but hang tight. All I ask is that you stay open to the suggestions. At times you may completely disagree with what I'm teaching. In fact, I'm sure you will. Most of what you'll learn in this book is the opposite of what you've been conditioned to believe. But that's cool. New ideas are what you need. Clearly your old ways haven't been working. I'm here to teach you that life doesn't have to be tough, that you don't need to feel alone, and that miracles are your birthright. So be willing to see things differently and you'll be led to all the happiness and serenity that you desire. I know this is a pretty ballsy statement, but I'll straight-up testify to it. As it says in the Course, "There is a way of living in the world that is not here, although it seems to be. You do not change appearance, though you smile more frequently. Your forehead is serene; your eyes are quiet." Sounds totally awesome, right? Well, it is.

In this chapter I'll start us off on our journey by introducing the key principles of the Course, which identify fear as an illusion and a shift in perception as a miracle. For the most part, I'll be sticking to the Course's language, but from time to time I'll Gabbify some stuff. I'll begin by reminding you of the state of mind we were born with, which I'll refer to as "love." Here, I'll take you back in time to the peace you once knew as an innocent child. Then I'll identify the key reasons you're no longer grooving in that way. I'll guide you to understand what the *Course* teaches is a major reason that we sink into unhappiness, which, simply put, is a separation from our inner state of joy. Then, I'll wrap up the chapter with an exercise designed to help you identify the negative thought patterns you've created in your mind. Taking inventory of those patterns is the first move toward shifting them. Our journey will begin with "love." What better way to start!

Born in Love

The love I'll speak of throughout the book is not to be confused with romantic love. The *Course* defines love as *"the right-minded emotion of peace and joy."* This kind of love is not something we offer to some people and deny others— this is one love that embodies everything and everyone. When we're in a state of love we see everyone as equal and we feel at ease all the time. This state is fearless and faithful.

Love is where we all begin. When we are born, all we know is love. Our *~ing* is on! (If you haven't read my last book, *Add More ~ing to Your Life*, allow me to translate: *~ing* is your inner guide, which is the voice of intuition, inspiration, and love. Throughout the book I'll refer to love, spirit, and ~*ing* interchangeably.) Our thoughts are aligned with love and our minds are peaceful. Our loving mind believes that all people are equal and that we are part of something larger than ourselves. We believe that we are supported and connected to everything everywhere. We believe that only love is real. We believe in miracles.

When I was first exposed to this lesson from the *Course*, it was hard for me to remember a time from my past when love fully ran the show. Even as a young child I felt anxious and skittish, and as if something were off-kilter. When I had that fleeting encounter with love during my early meditation days, I knew for sure that the presence of love was missing as a constant in my life. In that fleeting moment during my meditation, I felt it and it was real. Although I was unable to capture it and pin it down at the time, I was able to hang on to its memory for some sense of serenity.

A Tiny Mad Idea

So we are born into love, and then pretty soon thereafter fear is introduced. We begin to pick up the fear around us and are led to deny love. One tiny mad idea can hijack our loving mindset, and as the *Course* says, "*we forgot to laugh.*" This tiny mad idea could have arrived as early as infancy. Maybe Mom was anxious or Dad yelled a lot. As innocent babies we pick up fear from the outside world. All it takes is one tiny mad idea to make us detour into fear. A thought like "I'm not smart enough," or "Daddy doesn't like me, because he left," or "I'm not pretty enough" can separate us from love. The moment we take this tiny mad idea seriously, we get caught in a nightmare and forget to wake up.

With one fearful thought we lose love and are thereby separated from our ~*ing*. This is what the *Course* calls "dissociation," which it basically defines as "*a decision to forget.*" We chose to forget that we were equally as loveable and worthy as everyone and everything everywhere. Instead we chose to believe in fear and to perceive ourselves as separate in all ways. In some cases we believe we are better than others and special, whereas in other instances we believe we aren't good enough and are lesser-than. This thinking is destructive and unproductive: it leads us nowhere fast.

The tiny mad idea that totally seized my ~*ing* arrived when I was eight years old and landed a national TV commercial. This was monumental, not because I was proud of my acting or excited about being on TV, but because it was the first time I remember my father ever noticing me. It's not that my father was a mean man or a bad parent; it's just that I don't remember having much of a connection with him when I was young. Then, once I got a taste of what his attention felt like, it became like a drug that I couldn't get enough of. From that point forward, I was on the chase for more. I became a love junkie.

Though I didn't realize it, that experience began to reprogram my mind. It taught me that outward success equals "Daddy loves me," and that I wasn't good enough without his attention. So I continued to do whatever it took to be noticed. That was when I *detoured into fear*. This one tiny mad idea became my root issue, and a whacked-out emotional blueprint was set down to be built upon for the next twenty years of my life. I lost my faith in love and fell for the fear instead.

The Ego

Upon learning of the tiny mad idea, we have two choices. As the *Course* says, *"You cannot be faithful to two masters who ask conflicting things of you."* Therefore we have to choose between the tiny mad idea and the love we came from. Most of the time we choose fear. This choice splits off our mind into another way of thinking, which the *Course* calls the "ego." (This is not to be confused with the ego of psychology.) In an instant we are separated from love and allow the ego to take over. The ego becomes like a bully in our minds. The ego's goal is to shut down the love parade and trap us on a dark and lonely street by making us believe we're separate from the loving mindset we were born with. The ego cannot survive in the light of our loving mind, so it will do whatever it takes to keep the light off. When referencing the ego, the *Course* states, *"Listen to what the ego says, and see what it directs you to see, and it is sure that you will see yourself as tiny, vulnerable and afraid. You will experience depression, a sense of worthlessness, and feelings of impermanence and unreality.*" This lesson from the *Course* explained my deep-rooted anxiety and belief that I wasn't good enough. My loving mind had been captured by my ego.

The ego's sole purpose is to convince us that love isn't real so that we believe in the fearful thinking of the world. The ego is always revving up its game to take us down in a major way.

The *Course* says that "*the ego is totally confused and totally confusing.*" To keep us in the dark, the ego separates us from love. We're persuaded to deny love by believing in issues around body image, relationships, career, low self-esteem, and so on. As an adolescent I chose to be faithful to the ego. I was totally obsessed with what other people thought of me, who I was friends with, and what I looked like. My moment-to-moment thoughts were consumed with fear about these issues. From childhood up until my late twenties I cannot remember a time when my mind was free of fear. To make matters worse, I was obsessed with the coolness of the girls in the popular crowd and with how uncool I seemed to be by comparison. I chose to see those girls as separate from and better than me. The ego convinces us that we are better or worse than everyone around us. The ego's illusion convinces us to believe thoughts like "I'm not good enough to get into that school," or "I'm incomplete without a man," or "I'm way more popular than that girl." Deep down we know these thoughts are false, but we believe in them nonetheless.

To further keep us in the dark, the ego's illusion leads us to attack others and ourselves. In my case, because I felt so misunderstood and disconnected from my contemporaries, my ego convinced me that *they* were the problem: "They don't get me. They're just a bunch of assholes." My ego made everyone else wrong, which made me the victim. The ego loves to make victims of us.

Projection Makes Perception

The ego's main job is to make sure we don't change our mind about fear. The fearful projection that the ego inflicts on us becomes what we perceive to be our reality. As it says in the *Course*, *"The world you see is an outside picture of an inward condition."* When we choose the ego's projection of sin, guilt, anger, attack, and fear, that's all we'll perceive. It's a nightmare. The *Course* states, *"Perception is a choice and not a fact."* My projection of the ego became my perception in many areas of my life—especially when it came to my romantic relationships. Because I chose the ego thought that I'm not good enough without my father's attention, I later projected that thinking onto all my relationships with men. Projecting this tiny mad idea onto all my romantic partners led me to perceive myself as less-than and not good enough. This led me to do whatever I could to hold on to a romantic partner because without him I believed I was incomplete.

We all have our own individual projections and perceptions. For instance, two different people get upset after watching a TV show together. Even though they watched the same show, they're upset for different reasons. One person is upset over the romantic struggles of the characters, whereas the other person is worked up over the violence. Each person was projecting their own ego onto the television show, and therefore perceived what they chose to project. *Choice* is the operative word. That's right: we *choose* to believe in this crazy shit. We choose to project ideas like "I'm too fat," "I'm unworthy," and "I'm just not smart." We made a decision to forget about love and we fell for the mad idea instead. As a result, we live in a world that is based on these limiting projections. We project these thoughts and therefore perceive them to be real. Worst of all, we believe deeply in our perceptions because we're the ones who put them there.

Starting early in life, we project a belief system based on grades, cliques, bullies, and societal crap about body image. We have no choice but to ignore our ~*ing* because the voice of love cannot coexist with fear. Fear spreads like a virus, contaminating our minds. All it takes is one tiny mad idea to separate our mind from love and create a pattern of thinking in which fear always wins.

The ego also re-creates your past fears in the present. This was totally the case for me. My fear of not being good enough without male attention became my Achilles' heel and affected nearly every area of my life. I did whatever it took to attain male approval. I spent years trying to prove myself to my father in order to feel good enough. I'd come home with stories of my daily accomplishments and speak loudly to make sure I was heard. I desperately needed to be acknowledged by him to feel safe. My father loved me and approved of me of regardless of my outside accomplishments, but on the inside I believed the opposite.

The ego is crafty. There are a number of tricks the ego turns to in order to keep us in the dark, such as causing us to believe that others are more special than we are, causing us to attack others, or getting us into the nasty habits of denying our greatness and believing we are inadequate. Each trick convinces us to believe in fear and forget about love. Eventually we get so hooked into the ego's illusion that we cannot remember the loving mind we came from. It's as if we've been roofied by the ego.

This sounds seriously effed-up, right? Of course it does, but in one or more ways we've all fallen for the ego's mad idea. One fearful thought takes over our minds and creates our very own illusions. We were all innocent children who once believed in love. But there comes a point at which we forget love ever existed. We choose fear instead. We fear just about everything. We fear our careers, our family, our friends—we even fear the possibility that love could be real. Most of all we fear our own greatness.

The truthful voice of our *~ing* can only comprehend love. But because our minds detoured into fear, love became an afterthought. Our *~ing* became a mere murmur in the midst of the ego's inner riot. I can safely say that the majority of people I know have more faith in fear than in love. My life-coaching clients often say things like "I know there is a better way, but I just can't find it." Deep down we remember that all the love we need is inside us, but the ego's darkness has smothered that luminous truth.

You need to take a look at the wreckage from your past to understand fully how to transform the ego's patterns. Accepting the fact that you chose fear and turned your back on love is the first step. Don't beat yourself up about this. You couldn't have known any better and you've been doing the best you can to cope with the ego's projections for your entire life. But now it's time to fully understand what went down in order to create change.

Please know that even if you've forgotten about love, it never actually left you. Your mind just separated from it. This separation ignited the spark that became the fire that burns through your loving mind. Unfortunately, you chose to detour into Fear Land when you took sides with the ego and turned your back on love. I'm here to remind you that the separation was merely a choice, and that you can choose differently now.

The Ego Isn't Real

Over time, fear becomes our companion. The ego goes wild, taking over the loving part of our minds and convincing us of what the *Course* calls "the real world." The ego's real world is the illusory nightmare that we've bought into. My "real world" was based on a belief system of being alone, separate, and incomplete without a romantic partner. I also believed that I wasn't smart and had nothing to offer the world. My ego projected my world as small and rigidly limited.

The world that the ego creates for all of us is based on belief in sin, attack, fear, competition, lack, sickness, and so on. The ego convinces us that we're all a bunch of separate bodies out to make more money, find a better spouse, or look better than the next person. None of this is real. It's all an illusion that our ego creates in our minds and repeats enough so that we believe in it. The repetition of the ego's illusion becomes a bad dream that we reinforce with every fear-based idea. We've saved our faith for fear. But deep inside each of us lives a soft voice reminding us that love is real.

The First Step out of the Ego's World of Illusion

The only problems we have are the thoughts we project. What's happened is that we think these funky thoughts enough times that we believe them to be true. Then the thoughts create anxiety, fear, anger, attack, and guilt. By recognizing that the thought isn't real we can release the perception. We must understand that the thought is something we created a long time ago and that we've just projected it onto our present and future.

Recognizing that the ego's projections are illusions is the first step to restoring your mind back to love. This was major for me. When I first began practicing the *Course*, I was relieved to witness my projections. By looking closely at my fears, I was able to stop perceiving them as real. For instance, when I wrote my first book, *Add More ~ing to Your Life*, I was rocked by the ego at first. All my childhood beliefs of not being smart enough rose to the surface. My ego said things like "Who are you to write a book? You're just a stupid girl with the writing skills of an eighth grader." By that point I was already practicing the *Course* and was therefore able to witness that these fearful thoughts were based on an illusion of being stupid that I'd picked up in sixth grade. I witnessed the fearful thought without judgment and was therefore able to weaken its power and write an awesome book!

I want these messages to sink in, and I hope to guide you to see how the ego has played a role in your own nightmare. At this point in the process, let's shine light on your own tiny mad ideas.

Negative Thought Pattern Exercise

With eyes closed, think of the negative thought patterns that cross your mind. Name each one as it occurs to you, and then call it out. Deny its reality by following the fearful thought with the loving response, *"Love did not create it, and so it is not real."*

>   *Examples:*
>   Ego thought: *I am unworthy of happiness.*
>   Loving response: *Love did not create the belief*
>   *that I'm unworthy, and so it is not real.*
>   Ego thought: *I can't make money.*
>   Loving response: *Love did not create lack, and*
>   *so it is not real.*

This exercise might not make sense to you at first. Throughout the text, the *Course* acknowledges that you may not fully understand the concepts it introduces at first, but teaches you to continue forward nonetheless. The *Course* states, *"The exercises are very simple. They do not require a great deal of time, and it does not matter where you do them. They need no preparation."* Therefore, all you need is an open mind and the willingness to be guided.

With your newfound willingness we'll move on to chapter 2, where we'll look more closely at the ego's illusion. Hang tight and know that each simple shift in perception creates miraculous change.

Quick Review

- We are all born into a state of love, in which we see everyone as equal.

- One tiny mad idea can hijack our loving mindset. We choose fear instead of love.

- This choice splits off our mind into another way of thinking called the "ego." The ego's goal is to shut down the love parade and keep us in the dark by making us believe we're separate from the loving mindset we were born with.

- The repetition of the ego's illusion becomes a bad dream that we reinforce with every fear-based idea. But deep inside each of us lives a soft voice reminding us that love is real.

- Recognizing that the ego's projections are false illusions is the first step to restoring our mind back to love.

2
Anxiety and Ashrams

What is joyful to you is painful to the ego.

—A COURSE IN MIRACLES

Flashback to my teenage years. The tiny mad idea that had grabbed hold of me when I was eight took over and my anxiety got progressively worse. In an effort to help, my mother brought me to visit the ashram in South Fallsburg, New York, where her guru taught. At that point I was willing to do whatever it took to find some peace of mind. As we pulled into the ashram grounds, I saw people smiling with peaceful expressions on their faces. I felt a rush of love come over me, much like the experience I had while meditating. People smiled as we drove by them. Their eyes sparkled with a sense of lightheartedness and freedom. Then my body began to tingle and my hands went numb. I didn't speak up about what I was experiencing; I just allowed it to wash over me. In these new surroundings, I felt a sense of safety engulf me. Everything looked brighter here. It was like I was awake in a dream.

But the sensation was fleeting; as soon as we parked and began walking toward the main buildings, my anxiety returned. A voice in the back of my mind said, *That feeling was too good to be true. Nice try, sister!* As soon as I

heard the taunt of the familiar voice, my anxiety intensified. It was even worse than usual. I was experiencing an
overwhelming sadness, tightness in my chest, and panic for
fear that the sensation wouldn't go away. After only half
an hour spent walking through the ashram witnessing the
people, sitting in the meditation room, and getting accli-
mated, I couldn't bear my anxiety. I made my mother take
me home.

When we got into the car, my mother explained that I
was like a sponge soaking up the energy around me. That
was the reason my feeling of anxiety seemed even worse
than usual: I was not only reacting to the fear, but absorb-
ing the intense energy within the ashram itself. She went
on to say that this openness was a gift, but because I didn't
know how to control it, it left me unsettled and flustered.
Spiritual places like ashrams often attract people who
are not well and are in search of healing, she explained.
Because I was already in a fearful head-space, I was likely
to have picked up the anxiety of the others around me. My
ego met their egos, which compounded my own fear. So
not only was I totally freaked out about my own issues, but
I had picked up other people's fears, too. The entire experience infuriated me, and I began attacking my mother's
belief system. I was over her New Age approach to serenity,
I told her. It was time for me to take matters into my own
hands.

Numbing Out

In order to avoid my anxiety and fear, I reasoned that I had to anesthetize myself. So I rolled a joint and drank a beer. This remedy worked until one blowout night when it became clear that alcohol and drugs took me to some scary places.

My mother had gone out of town and left me home alone with my brother. You can probably guess where I'm going here. Yup, I threw a small gathering of thirty of my closest friends. As usual, we drank beer and smoked weed—nothing out of the ordinary. Then the paranoia set in. This didn't seem to be the typical pot-smoking paranoia. It was a whole other monster. I was crawling out of my skin. I felt overcome by fear and an underlying sense of guilt. I felt like I'd done something terribly wrong. This guilt/paranoia/anxiety cocktail was too much. I ended up kicking everyone out.

I called my mom the next day and told her what had happened. I felt safer outing my problems than hiding them. Her immediate response was "I expected this call." She went on to tell me that on the day of my party she'd gone to see an astrological reader. When she asked about me, the reader made a strong suggestion that I never use drugs or alcohol. The reader said that I was a very sensitive being and that I had a lot of psychic energy. She suggested that drugs and alcohol would take me to a place I didn't need to go, and that I'd struggle with this for some time.

I was surprised that drugs and alcohol had that effect on me. But my experience at the ashram and the astrologer's prophecies didn't make anything less crazy in my mind. In fact, I felt worse. I now perceived myself as a freak, soaking up the energy of others and unable to handle my liquor. This perception reinforced my feeling of being an outsider.

The Crafty Ego

In retrospect I can clearly see the craftiness of my ego back then. While at the ashram, my ego had sensed love coming over me when I first arrived. My ego couldn't survive in the light of this love, so it had to deny it to keep me in the dark. The ego can only survive when we're in pain. As the *Course* teaches, *"No one desires pain. But he can think that pain is pleasure. No one would avoid his happiness. But he can think that joy is painful, threatening and dangerous."* What I didn't realize at the time was that my ego had convinced me that "joy is painful," thereby weakening my faith in love. My ego had several nasty tricks at its disposal to keep me stuck in the illusion that my pain had purpose.

Remember, the ego is like a bully that takes over our minds. As soon as the ego sensed my mother's attempts to reconnect me with love, it bullied me into siding with fear to resist her efforts. My ego barged in to say, "Come on, Gab, that feeling of love is too good to be true. Don't believe your mom's hippie shit. That ain't real."

The Ego's Bag of Tricks

The ego totes around its bag of tricks in the same way we carry a favorite clutch. This bag holds space for what the *Course* refers to as the ego's "friends," namely sin, guilt, fear, denial, and attack. Whenever we start thinking loving thoughts, our ego reaches into its bag. The ego grabs on tightly to one of its "friends" to drag us back into fear. The ego reaches into the bag when it needs to defend against love.

Each trick is cunning and baffling. The *Course* says, *"The ego vacillates between suspiciousness and viciousness."* In order to overcome the ego's stronghold, we must understand its ways, so in this chapter we'll take a thorough look at the ego's crafty tricks. I'll guide you to witness the ego's commitment to keeping us in the dark. This will help you differentiate your ego from the loving voice of your ~ing and give you more power to change your fearful patterns. The *Course* teaches that we must acknowledge our misery so that we can begin to change it.

The goal of this chapter is to guide you to understand

how the ego works. Toward that end, I've outlined the ego's tricks for you one by one. Use this breakdown as a guide, as these tricks will continue to come up throughout your journey inward.

The Nasty Tricks That Keep the Ego Alive

The moment at the ashram when love settled in, my ego freaked out. Remember that the ego cannot survive in the light of loving thoughts. If I'd chosen love, the ego couldn't endure. As it says in the *Course*, "*Whenever light enters darkness, the darkness is abolished.*" Therefore, the ego had to rev up its game and hook me back into fear. In order to keep me in the dark the ego reached into its bag of tricks. The ego's tricks convinced me to fear love.

Fear

One of the ego's first-line tools is fear. Fear was the primary feeling I experienced in my life before I began my *Course* work. At the time I couldn't actually express why I was afraid, but I felt fearful all the time. That fear is what led me to try to numb out with drugs and alcohol. The *Course* says, "*Being afraid seems to be involuntary; something beyond your own control.*" Fear is often a sign that you've turned your back on love and chosen to have faith in the ego.

Today I realize I was fearful back then for a few reasons. The first reason was entirely buried in my subconscious. I was afraid that I'd lost something—that I'd lost love. The voice of love had been beckoning me through moments of positive self-talk and the deep desire to perceive the world from a happier perspective, but time and time again I was tempted back to fear. By choosing the ego, I'd denied love altogether. This ignited an unconscious horrifying thought that I'd killed love forever. And the fleeting encounters with love that I found through meditation and at the ashram actually created more fear. Because my ego mind had become more powerful than love, I was afraid I'd lost love altogether. This fear led me into a deep depression. And what I feared most was that I would never get out of it.

The second reason for my fear was based on my own conscious decisions. I'd chosen to believe in fear. I'd chosen to believe in the ego's separate thinking that I was a girl living in a world of attack, war, separateness, anger, and discomfort. I was afraid of this world because it was the opposite of the love I remembered and because it was straight-up scary! I turned my back on love altogether and chose to believe this projected world was real. In other words, I chose to live in fear.

Fear of the Past

This world I'd projected was based on fearful past experiences that my ego clung on to—experiences of not feeling good enough, smart enough, pretty enough, thin enough. Things as simple as being told I was stupid or having acne were ways for the ego to run roughshod over my mind. My ego pulled these past experiences into the present moment and made them real over and over again.

I'd relive my past experiences daily. For instance, in middle school I was bullied. This experience of being attacked by others created a dark corner in my mind where I believed I wasn't good enough. I established a belief system in which the mean girls were better than I was. I carried this experience with me into high school. As a result of the belief system I had established, I was afraid of many of my female contemporaries and never found a true group of friends. I relived the experience of having been bullied in middle school daily when I walked through the halls in high school, felt alone in the lunch room, and sat in the front of the bus on school trips. This middle-school bullying gave my ego fuel to fire up a belief system based on separation, unworthiness, and lack. By bringing the past into the present, the ego stayed alive.

Fear of the Future

Once the ego has convinced you that the fear of the past is real in the present, it then hooks you into the future. I was so afraid of the present moment that I began to project more fear onto the future. I was totally freaked out about going to college because as it was I was barely able to make friends in high school. This fear-based thinking, which dated back to being bullied in middle school, was brought into the present and projected onto a future college experience that didn't even exist yet. Projecting fear onto the future is another way for the ego to control your mind. Future-tripping is totally whacked out because the ego convinces you to project forward to attempt to control future outcomes. None of this is real. No one can control the future because it doesn't exist. However, it's a sneaky ego trick that will hook you into fear time and time again.

Self-Attack

In addition to my past- and future-tripping, I also got great at letting my ego attack me. In order to keep me in the dark my ego led me to attack myself and feel pain on a moment-by-moment basis. Self-inflicted pain is perhaps the sharpest kind of pain there is, and it makes me cringe just to think about it. I spent years attacking myself in my mind and in my actions: overeating, making poor and impulsive choices, judging myself or telling myself I sucked and that I was unlovable. Using drugs and alcohol only fired up the ego even more.

The ego uses self-attack to ensure that we feel pain. The *Course* teaches that if there is pain there is no love. Our egos have a tremendous need to hurt us in order to prove that we suffer and keep us believing in pain. As long as we're suffering, we see ourselves as separate from love, and the ego remains real.

Attacking Others

To make matters worse, the ego starts attacking others. Whenever we feel threatened or hurt by someone, rather than forgive them and remember that they're love, too, the ego will "protect" us from hurt by attacking. This "protection" is actually another ego trick for keeping the illusion alive. As long as we're attacking someone, we're reinforcing fear, anger, resentment, and lack of forgiveness. This is a funky trick because the ego has convinced us that this attack is "protection." Actually, the attack only makes us feel worse because we're deepening the illusion and strengthening the ego's separation.

Attack Thoughts

Attack goes on in our actions and, even worse, in our minds. I began to believe in attack thoughts of separation such as "She's only cool because her family is rich," or "My mom's a crazy hippie who doesn't understand my tortured reality," or "I don't need a clique because I'm better than them." By attacking others I felt as though I were protecting myself. Meanwhile, the only things I was protecting were my ego's illusions. Each time I'd gossip, feel jealous, or think nasty thoughts, I was attacking others and deepening my faith in fear.

The Problem

The problem was not something on the outside; the problem was in my mind. The *Course* says, *"It is your thoughts alone that cause you pain."* The problem isn't what's in the ego's bag of tricks, but that I chose to reach for the bag in the first place. Why did I reach for it? Because I forgot there was another way. The ego had worked so hard to convince me to believe in fear that I'd forgotten that love was an option. I had no idea why I was so uncomfortable and upset, so I grabbed the bag of tricks to find a solution. I'd reach for the ego's tricks to deny love by attacking others in an attempt to protect myself and keep the ego alive.

Wow, I can only imagine how heady this must sound to you. Hang tight. Rather than overthink these new concepts, just let the upcoming tools guide you. It is important that you don't judge the ego. A *Course in Miracles* spends a lot of time instructing us to look at the ego and not underestimate its viciousness. In fact, what you learn about the ego can be quite terrifying. As you begin watching your own thoughts, you see the ego everywhere. Don't freak out. Remember that the ego has had all of us in a headlock—you're not alone. Just witness the ego's tricks without judgment. The *Course* teaches us not to be afraid of the ego. It says that the ego *wants* us to be afraid of its thoughts; being afraid of the ego makes us believe in it. The *Course* teaches that the only power the ego has is the power we give it. The source of the ego's strength is in our mind.

This is reinforced in lesson five in the *Course* workbook, which teaches, *"I'm never upset for the reason I think."* Our problems are not the issues of the world that we choose to believe in, or the people we attack. Our problem is that we choose to deny love. In fact, we only have one problem: that our mind chooses fear over love.

In this first section of the book, I'm your guide to taking a good look at how the ego took over your mind. It is imperative that you understand what went down. The first step is recognizing that things are not working. If you find yourself saying "I'm not happy," then you're in the right place. The work of looking closely at the ego's tricks will help you see how the thoughts you've chosen to believe work to create what you perceive as your reality.

By fighting, suffocating, or trying to obliterate the ego we just make it more real. All you need to do at this point is witness. Take it one step at a time. By witnessing the shadiness of the ego you'll take one more step toward setting yourself free.

In this chapter your only job is to focus on how the ego's tricks have wreaked havoc. By witnessing the ego in action you'll begin to see how your mind has separated from love. Taking an inventory of this separation will help you understand how much of your fear isn't real—that your fears are delusional thoughts created by your ego. This step will guide you to begin to slowly disassociate from the fears you've come to believe in. By seeing that your fears stem from the ego's tricks you'll have a whole new perspective.

Examining Your Ego

Before we begin the exercise below, I want to be clear that I'm not suggesting you attack the ego. Once again, the problem isn't the ego; the problem is your *belief* in the ego. But don't judge yourself for choosing fear. You couldn't have known any better.

Now it's time to take a good look at how the ego has worked to keep you stuck in that illusion. This will be our first step in the undoing of the ego. You'll begin by asking yourself a series of questions to become more aware of the ego's presence in your life. This is followed by a freewriting exercise that throughout the book I'll refer to as an ~ing-write (inner guidance writing). You'll ~ing-write each of your responses in a journal. Take your time doing this writing exercise. Allow your subconscious to come forward and try to be aware when it attempts a retreat.

The next step will be to take a daily inventory of your ego, acknowledging its trickster ways. Your ego will be weakened each time you acknowledge its tricks because when you look at darkness without judgment, you shine light on it. This is detrimental to the ego because it cannot survive in the light. Our work together isn't about blasting light onto the ego overnight, but rather one day at a time *shining* light on the darkness of the ego to reconnect with love. Therefore, be patient and committed to becoming aware of how the ego has played a role in your illusion.

Take a Close Look

The work in this exercise will guide you to become honest about how the ego has been playing tricks in your mind. Before you begin to take an inventory of the ego, let's start with a meditation. Looking directly at the ego can be scary because the ego is afraid of being found out. Therefore, in this meditation I will prepare you to witness your ego's patterns clearly and without fear. Immediately following the meditation, answer the questions below. Trust that your

Witnessing Meditation
(For the audio version, visit www.gabbyb.tv/meditate.)

Sit up straight in your chair, with your feet planted firmly on the ground.

Gently breathe in through your nose and out through your mouth.

Breathe in: I welcome guidance.

Breathe out: I am willing to see the truth.

Breathe in: I am fearless.

Breathe out: I release attack.

Breathe in: I let go of the past.

Breathe out: I release the future.

Breathe in: I welcome the present moment.

Breathe out: I allow my inner guide to lead me to what is real.

meditation will take the edge off and lead you to truthful responses.

Gently open your eyes to the room and answer the following questions:

1. *What am I afraid of?*
~ing-write your response . . .

2. *How do I attack myself?*
~ing-write your response . . .

3. *How do I attack others?*
~ing-write your response . . .

4. *How do I bring my past fears into the present and future?*
~ing-write your response . . .

Spot-Check Your Ego

For a week or more, spot-check your ego throughout the day. Take a small notebook with you and, on the hour, every hour, take a fearless inventory of your ego.

Every hour, write in your journal the answers to these questions:

> Did I deny love, and how?
> Did I attack, and whom?
> Was I fearful? What was I fearful of?

Remember not to judge yourself for having these projections. Once again, you've been doing the best you can with a lot of fear thrown in your lap. Just continue to witness your ego in action and have faith in my plan. Know that I've got your back. In the coming chapters you'll receive beautiful tools for releasing the pain and suffering of the ego. Right now, though, it's all about becoming aware and acknowledging the pain. This may in itself bring you some peace of mind. When I began to perceive my fear as created by the ego rather than by my true self, I immediately started to feel better.

Reflecting

The process of reflecting on the ego's crafty work is very powerful. Understanding the ego's tricks will help you move forward. At times you may get confused. That is to be expected. Remember, we're reconditioning years of thinking. You've probably become so accustomed to the ways of the ego that you believe they are real. In fact, I'm pretty confident that's the case. Your ego likely has convinced you that your problems are your reality. Therefore, you may hear your ego's voice inside say, *This is craziness. What does she mean, my fear isn't real? Isn't the drama at my job real? Aren't those mean girls real? Isn't the fact that I hate my mother real?*

Of course this will be your response, because the world of these fearful thoughts is what you believe in. But I'm here to guide you gently to detach from these worldly fears and begin to see in a different way. My work is to help you see that these fear-based "realities" around you are simply choices you made. They are blocks to love.

Remember that our work together is not based on finding love on the outside. Instead, our work is to release the blocks to the awareness of love's presence on the inside. So be fearless about this inventory. Look closely and stay honest. Get clear about the blocks so you can begin to remove them. On this journey, one day at a time you will remove these blocks as I guide you to remember love. The *Course* says, "*Children perceive frightening ghosts and monsters and dragons, and they are terrified. Yet if they ask someone they trust for the meaning of what they perceive, and are willing to let their own interpretations go in favor of reality, their fear goes with them. When a child is helped to translate his 'ghosts' into a curtain, his 'monster' into a shadow, and his 'dragon' into a dream he is no longer afraid, and laughs happily at his own fear.*"

Each time we acknowledge that there must be a better way, our loving mind can begin to intervene. When we recognize the ego's role in our unhappiness, we invite love in to intervene. We must not look at our ego with judgment. Instead, we must begin to see our fear as a curtain rather than a ghost.

Be proud of yourself for taking this fearless inventory. Each time you witness the ego in action, you can perceive it as separate from you. Seeing your ego as a separate entity reminds you that you are not your fear. When you recognize that *you are not your ego*, you become more connected to your loving spirit. Lifting the curtain of fear takes guts, and I'm here to guide you through each step. In chapter 3 we'll boldly examine one of the ego's craftiest tricks: the "special relationship." Stay committed to this process, knowing that with each exercise we are one step closer to removing the blocks to your loving connection with the spirit within you.

3
Somethin' Special

The special love relationship is the ego's chief

weapon for keeping you from Heaven.

—A COURSE IN MIRACLES

◆

My First Idol

In high school I fell hard for the ego's mad idea. I was consumed by fear. As a result, I often felt unsafe when I was alone. I was on an endless search for solace in someone or something outside of myself. My mother often said to me, "Why can't you spend time alone? Can't you read a book and be by yourself?" Little did she know that I was afraid to be alone. When I was by myself, I had nothing to distract me from my anxiety and fearful thoughts. I'd hide out in someone else's reality so that I didn't have to deal with my own. To be super clear, it's not that I had a bad life in any way. In fact, on the outside it was all good. I had a great family, a nice home, friends, and all the trappings of what it takes to be happy, but on the inside I was a complete mess. I felt like Dorothy following the Yellow Brick Road in search of a wizard to save me.

When I was sixteen, I found him.

He drove a silver Beetle with black lightning bolts streaking down each side. The speakers and the clutch were lit up in blue neon. No joke, blue neon. He had a golden afro and sported a white tank top with belled-out jeans. He tattooed our astrological signs side by side on his thigh. His sign, Sagittarius; mine, Scorpio. He was a second-generation Arab Muslim dating me, a Jewish girl from the 'burbs.

I'm sharing this experience with you in an effort to teach you the meaning of idols. From the *Course's* perspective, an idol is someone you make better than yourself, your friends, and your family. You believe your idol is your source of happiness. So *he* was my first idol, and man, did I dig him. He became my *everything*. He was my lunch buddy, my social life, my dance partner, my prom date, and my best friend. He was *it*. On his end, the only thing he loved as much as me was his band. They wore silver sequined jumpsuits and played a hybrid of ska and electronica. And like any good groupie I became one with the band. I'd do anything for him.

I thought he was incredible. I remember waking up on Valentine's Day to my mother screaming from the living room of our sixth-floor apartment. "Look out the window!" she yelled. I ran to the window to see that he had spray-painted a huge red heart in the snow. Inside the heart it read, "Happy Valentine's Gabrielle." I was living in a fairy tale.

This fairy tale lasted more than two years. Then he graduated, and my first idol fell. Nothing was the same after that. He went to college and was more interested in meeting new people and being away from home. He got totally hooked into college life and broke up with me. I was like Bella in *Twilight*. My Edward left me alone and I had nothing without him. And, much like Bella, without my boyfriend I was vulnerable to vampires. But in my case the vampires were in my mind. I remember staying in bed for weeks—maybe a month. I couldn't eat, sleep, or breathe. This love was my first drug, and now I had to come down from the high.

Something Special

Man, did I think he was special. In fact, this was my biggest problem in the relationship. I put him on a pedestal and turned him into an idol. I began to view him as above everyone else in my life (including myself). So I was completely devastated when he broke up with me. This act of turning someone into a worshiped idol is one of the craftiest tricks in the ego's grab bag. This trick in particular is what really took me down.

Throughout this chapter I'll offer up an understanding of how this trick furthers your belief in separateness and deepens the fearful illusion. I'll teach you about the "special love relationship" that the ego hooks you into with romantic partners. In addition, I'll show you how the ego makes all kinds of relationships and situations "special." You'll learn that this idolizing isn't all that special when you see its nasty effects. In fact, it is one of the ego's most powerful tools for keeping us stuck in the dark by separating us from others. Let's start with the "special love relationship."

The Special Love Relationship

When your source of happiness lives in the arms of another human being, you're totally screwed. The ego convinces us that all the love we need is in one "special" person. This is what the *Course* calls a "special love relationship." This kind of relationship differs from your other relationships in that you come to believe you need this person to be complete. The special love relationship is exclusive, and it makes that one special person better than you and everyone else.

My high school romance is the perfect example of the special love relationship. I made him my idol, my happiness, and my source of security in life. My ego convinced me that in his arms I would find all the serenity and happiness I was seeking. This was my ego's tool for keeping me stuck in the dark and away from my true source of inner love.

There is no way that special love can ever work. No one person can be your source of happiness. But without knowing where to find that true source, one will keep searching for it in all kinds of people, hoping to find *the one*. This was the case for me. The breakup only reinforced my limiting beliefs that I was unsafe on my own, so I began a committed search for yet another "one special love." I believed the only possible way for me to recover from the loss of my first idol and the hole inside my heart was to fill it with another special relationship. Just as when Bella turned to Jacob to recover from Edward, I, too, found my werewolf.

For the next ten years I overlapped relationships to feel "safe." I was so afraid of being alone that I totally compromised my own needs to stay in a relationship. Remember that this pattern was based on my ego's tiny mad idea from childhood, that without male attention I wasn't good enough. The ego had convinced me that without a man I was incomplete and therefore unsafe, taking my fear from the past and projecting it onto the present. In retrospect, I can see that this fearful addiction was based on the ego's lies. The story wasn't real, but it sure as hell felt real at the time. I was convinced of it.

This fear lived deep inside my mind and took over my reality. It kept me clinging onto relationships that were totally wrong for me, for fear of being alone. In addition, the fear made me completely inauthentic and insecure. For more than a decade I lived in a delusional nightmare of codependency and a search for that "one special love."

The Romantic Illusion

Sound familiar? I bet it does. I'm confident that the concept of special love will resonate with many readers. Romantic relationships are the ego's playground, and nine times out of ten our ego will turn the chance of romantic bliss into a freakin' nightmare. The ego feeds us illusions. What often happens is that we create a completely delusional story in our mind of who this person is, and how amazing he or she is. We project all kinds of special ideas, such as "When I have that ring I'll be happy," "He is all I need," "I'm complete now that I have love." Yada yada yada.

To make matters worse, the ego has convinced us that we cannot live without a "special" partner. This need for a special partner is a primary cause of codependency. Such fear-based thinking leads us to do whatever it takes to make people happy so that they don't leave. We become inauthentic and subservient so that we don't lose our special relationship. We put the needs of others before of our own, and deny our true feelings. We do all this in the name of special love.

This ego behavior is totally manipulative and chaotic. I was a hundred percent caught up in these types of codependent patterns owing to my belief in special love. I would do whatever it took to keep a relationship alive, even when it was clearly no longer working. I'd dress a certain way, try to "be cool" all the time, and always play it off as though I were super easygoing. The worst part was that I'd put my "special love partner" before all my friends, family, and personal goals. I'd reschedule my plans, go far out of my way, and bend over backwards to make my special love partner happy. Ironically, all the behavior that I thought was keeping them was actually turning them off. My inability to be authentic, mixed with an underlying needy energy, was not very attractive. Consequently, these relationships never had a long shelf life.

When, inevitably, the relationship would end, I felt as though my life would end with it. I was so afraid to be alone that I'd do anything I could to get into another relationship. This fear lived deep inside my heart. It was so real to me at the time. I felt as though I would literally die if I were alone. My happiness, serenity, and peace relied on my relationship status.

Future-Tripping in the Illusion

The ego also uses future projections to hook us into the illusion. Often we project specialness onto someone we've just met. One wink, flirtatious text, or hint of affection will lead us down the ego's road of special future-tripping. Within minutes, in our imaginations we're walking down the aisle and decorating our home. The ego will grab any shred of attention we receive, and become addicted to it. Our ego has the capacity to convince us that someone we don't even know is super special. This is clearly a romantic illusion.

Special Doesn't Stop Here

My special projections didn't stop with romance. I made my work special, certain friends special, celebrities special, and on it went. I had certain friends I'd spend time with at the drop of a hat, whereas I couldn't be bothered to answer the phone when others called. These were all responses to how "cool" I thought other people were and how "cool" I'd be by association if I hung out with them. I placed all kinds of outward projections onto others, which fueled my ego's illusion that everyone was different and that some were more special than others.

The concept of "special" is based on anything we make an idol of—anything we perceive as better than others or ourselves. The ego has all kinds of ways of convincing us that people are special. When we perceive that someone is more special than others, we're thinking with separation. We've forgotten that we are all one, and we've hooked back into the ego's thought system of better-than and worse-than.

The nastiest special relationship is the one we have

with ourselves. To this day I have to work very hard to combat my ego's habit of talking about how damn special I think I am. Flaunting our own specialness is a sign we've been hangin' with the ego for too long. In one way or another we've all made ourselves more special than others. Possibly you see yourself as more special than the intern in your office, or the homeless person on the street, or your younger sibling. The world around us thrives on this separation of more special versus less special. It shows up everywhere.

I've also found that we can do a back-and-forth special dance. At some of my most insecure times I'd see a pretty, put-together woman on the street and think, "She's better than me because she's thin," or "She clearly has better style than I do and therefore more money because she can afford those shoes." Then I'd reverse the specialness by "protecting myself" with a nasty comeback such as, "Whatever, that's last year's handbag and she's actually not as thin as I thought. I'm prettier than she is anyway." This thinking would reverse the specialness back to me.

The Special Teacher

Another major way our culture has created specialness is through the teacher-student relationship. When I began following Marianne Williamson's work, I idolized her to the max. I saw her as this guru who knew it all. When I became friends with Marianne and forged a personal relationship with her, I carried along this thinking. In my first letter to Marianne, I admitted that I was working hard not to make an idol of her. My willingness to open up about my ego's thinking really helped me release a bit of the special projection. Outing the ego is empowering because we are reminded that it's a projection in our mind rather than our reality. I'm not gonna lie, though: I work on this daily. I adore Marianne dearly and I have a hard time not seeing her as a special idol. But when I reconnect to the work, I remember that the light I see in her is a reflection of the light I see in me.

We're All Special

The *Course* teaches that we're all special. This is hard for us to grasp at first. Because we've spent so many years perceiving others as better or worse than ourselves, we cannot possibly see ourselves as equal. We've become so accustomed to thinking with separation that we have a hard time disassociating from the concept that everyone has an equal amount of awesomeness on the inside. This type of thinking gets people really tripped up at times.

"How Do I De-special a Relationship?"

Relinquishing our special ties takes a serious commitment to change. I once received an e-mail from a client saying, "I've tried meditating, praying, and praying again, and I still cannot release this special relationship. I've made him a McSpecial with a side of fries. How do I de-special some-one?" I got a kick out of this e-mail. Her desire to *de-special* that one relationship was wonderful, but I explained to her that it's not about this one person in particular. The problem is our overall belief in the concept of specialness. I told her to take the focus off releasing this *one person* and begin to commit to releasing all the people she's made special. I guided her to witness the ego in action when-ever the illusion of specialness came up. Her work was to take an inventory of whom and what she'd made spe-cial, including herself. Then I asked her to commit to a moment-by-moment perceptual shift of choosing to release the illusion of specialness.

No one can be expected to release the illusion of spe-cialness overnight; therefore I guided her to understand that this was a long-term goal that would require daily practice and dedication. The goal of the exercises in this chapter is to help you recognize how the ego's special trick has separated you from others. By looking closely at your special illusions, you'll once again expose the ego to the light. If you're ready to take another stab at releasing your ego's illusion, check out the suggested steps for releasing the special relationships.

"DE-SPECIAL" STEP 1. WHOM HAVE YOU MADE SPECIAL?

The first step to relinquishing the ego's projection of specialness is to spot-check whom you've made special. This step is dedicated to taking a daily inventory of your ego's special projections. Look closely at whom and what you've made special. Ask yourself: Whom have I made the most special, and how? Maybe you've made your boyfriend special, or your teacher, or a celebrity. You can also look at how you've idolized certain things other than people, such as a job, a career path, or an ideal weight. Use your journal and write out all the ways you've created special relationships within your life. Shine light on those special relationships and make a list of your top ten. Include yourself in the list if it applies.

"DE-SPECIAL" STEP 2. OUT IT

One of the most powerful ways to release your special projections (even temporarily) is to out them. For instance, when I admitted to Marianne that I'd been making an idol of her, I was able to release the ego's power. By merely acknowledging that I'd made her special, we were both able to laugh at the ego's mad idea and begin to release the projection.

Once you recognize where your ego has created special relationships, you can begin to call them out. Speak openly about how you've perceived others, and stay committed to seeing things differently. You may not want to tell your special relationships how special you think they are; instead, just share with your friends. By outing your ego to a friend, you weaken the ego's projection and begin to see others as equal.

"DE-SPECIAL" STEP 3. CHOOSE TO SEE IT DIFFERENTLY

Combating the ego is a choice. In all situations we have two choices: see with the ego or see with love. Each time you witness your special projections and say them out loud, you have a choice to defend them or release them. The ego will work hard to keep you in the dark by reinforcing the specialness in others and yourself. Therefore, it is important that you continue to choose to see equality in others.

You can bring this choice into your daily practice. Whenever you witness that you've made someone special, choose in that moment to see things differently. This simple mental shift will do all the work for you. The moment you choose to deny the ego, you invite in love. Say to yourself in that moment, "I choose to perceive this person as equal and know that the light in them is equal to the light in me."

In addition to practicing this mantra, you can use meditation as a tool for releasing specialness. Through mediation you can reconnect with the essence of all people rather than the projections that you've placed upon them. Follow my lead and allow yourself to release special illusions through the following meditation.

De-special Meditation
(For the audio version, visit www.gabbyb.tv/meditate.)

Sit up straight in your seat, with your palms facing upward.

Breathe gently in through your nose and out through your mouth.

Identify a person you have made special.

Imagine their body entering into the room with you.

Looking directly at them, witness a ball of golden light forming in their heart.

As you breathe in, welcome the light from their
heart into your heart.
On the exhalation, extend this light from your
heart to their heart.
Continue this cycle of breathing the light in and
out.
Breathe in the light from their heart.
Extend the light from your heart to their heart.
As the light extends, it begins to grow around
each of you.
As you continue breathing, the room is filled with
light.
The light surrounding both of you is a reminder
that you are one.
Breathe in: I see you as equal to me.
Breathe out: We are one in the light.
Breathe in: I release all specialness.
Breathe out: The light I see in you is equal to the
light in me.
Take one last breath in and open your eyes to the
room as you exhale.

This meditation is a powerful tool for reigniting your
inner belief in oneness. Each of us believes deep down that

we are all one. We know that specialness is just an illusion. We've just forgotten. Through meditation you can allow your inner guide to lead you to remember. Practice this meditation often to deepen your belief that we are all equally special.

Each time I call out the ego on the illusion, I weaken its strength. This is major work. Our ego has spent a lifetime convincing us of separateness and persuading us to believe in special forms of relationships. You may find yourself resisting this concept. That's cool. Just remember that whenever you make someone special you separate yourself from the opportunity to know true, connected love. You forget that we are all one.

I have to practice these tools often. I have a daily practice of releasing my special illusions, and I plan to be working on this until the illusions disappear. Who knows, it could take a lifetime. But regardless of how long it takes, I'm proud of the miraculous shifts I've already made.

As we continue on this journey together, I'll guide you to call on your ~ing often. Bring these three steps into all your lessons and know that your ~ing will lead the way. Relying on your inner guide is a major theme in the upcoming chapter as we begin to ask our ~ing for help. Turning to the help of your inner guide may seem difficult at first, but keep an open mind. Remember that the plan of the ego hasn't been working, and stay willing to see things in a new way. This willingness is all you need to allow spirit to help you out.

4
Ask~ing for Help

Trust not your good intentions. They are not
enough. But trust implicitly your willingness,
whatever else may enter.

—A COURSE IN MIRACLES

• ◆ •

In college I studied theater. This was the perfect major for me, because it let me escape from the world. Unable to find meaning in my own life, I chose to portray the lives of others. I didn't get it at the time, but the best actors are those who know themselves well—people who can travel deep into their own truth and bring forth their authenticity. I didn't even know what the word *authentic* meant back then: this led to a pretty difficult four years in a conservatory theater program.

During the first three years of theater school, I tried every which way to figure out how to make this degree program work for me. Finally, something got my attention. Third-year students were introduced to the Theater of the Absurd, a type of theatre developed in Paris during the 1950s. The work of the Absurdist playwrights expressed the belief that we live in a universe where human existence has no meaning, where attempts to assess our life's situation are absurd or essentially pointless. The Absurdist playwrights I studied focused on horrific or tragic images, characters caught in hopeless situations forced to carry out repetitive or meaningless actions, and plots that were cyclical or straight-up preposterous to our worldly minds. These characters resonated with me deeply. I was diggin' it. Playwrights such as Eugène Ionesco, Samuel Beckett, and Harold Pinter became my homeboys. I felt a deep connection to their work. These playwrights clearly had inner struggles going on, and their work made me feel as though I wasn't the only person wondering where we came from and why we were here.

I was still searching for meaning in my life. As I became more closely connected to Absurdist theater I realized that I'd become an actor on the stage that was my life. I was playing out archetypal roles that I thought were cool, acceptable, and worthy of acknowledgment. I now could see how my internal projector screen was showing the movie of my life. My connection to the Absurdist playwrights was another massive reminder that there was an existential way to view the world. I no longer felt alone in my inner beliefs. It was as if I'd been guided to their work.

More Denial

My college love affair with the Theater of the Absurd had a good run. Unfortunately, hiding out in the back of the theater reading Beckett had to come to an end. College graduation came and went, at which point I was tossed out into the "real world." I graduated in 2001, right after the dot-com bubble burst. Much like today, the economy had taken a turn for the worse. We were told that there were no jobs "out there" and to take whatever we could get. With a degree in theater and no desire to be an actress, I felt pretty lost. I interned, picked up odd jobs, and promoted parties to pay my bills. I continued to search for meaning in a seemingly meaningless reality.

Then, on September 11, 2001, things got way worse. I walked out of my apartment that morning to find people running north, covered in ash. I looked several blocks down Seventh Avenue and saw smoke pouring out of the World Trade Center. This was the end of the world as we knew it.

Like all New Yorkers, I have a story of where I was on 9/11. The horror of my story pales in comparison with the stories of people who were in the Twin Towers or who lost loved ones there, but it was an experience I'll never forget. Believe it or not, as much fear and terror as I saw that day, I saw an equal amount of love. The love I saw was overwhelming. Cabdrivers shepherded people uptown, neighbors acknowledged each other for the first time, strangers hugged on the street. Everyone was connected, it seemed. On that day our city released all separateness. No one was more special than anyone else. We were all one. There was so much fear around us that we had no other choice but to call on love for help. We prayed, lit candles, and prayed some more. We all turned to something greater than ourselves: we turned to love. I felt as though angels were looking down on us that day, smiling with pride as we turned to love for help.

I felt as though for a few months following 9/11 we held on to this way of being. People raised money, held hands, and took time off from their worldly priorities to be with family and friends. Then, when survival was no longer our concern, something seemed to shift. It felt as though as soon as we were slightly back on our feet, we forgot about love. At this point many of us turned to separation in a greater way than we'd known before, and ego ran riot. Politicians promoted spending, news anchors promoted fear, and racism took on a whole new form. Separation, attack, judgment, and fear were on fire.

In addition, many of us worked hard to numb our sadness. Like good New Yorkers, we drank, ate, and got back to work. Our "achieve" mentality was greater than ever. This was totally the case for me.

At this time, my ego's limiting beliefs spiked. In the wake of 9/11 I was living in the city, working odd jobs and single for the first time in years. In addition to the chaos surrounding me, I still grappled with the thought that I wasn't good enough unless I was in a romantic relationship or professionally successful. Since I was single, I felt as though I had to find another way to define myself. So I worked super hard to succeed in business. While all my friends were afraid not to have jobs, I was too afraid to have one. I needed to perceive myself as entrepreneurial in order to feel that I was doing something unique and remarkable. I needed a special identity. My drive for success was based on my ego's need to feel "special." So I jumped on the ego bandwagon and projected myself onto the world as a young entrepreneur.

I pulled together the skills I had acquired in theater school and in life. I was great with people and loved to promote things. This led me to position myself as a publicist. I'd been promoting parties at nightclubs for years, so I knew a thing or two about publicity. In addition, I could sell anything, thanks to my enthusiasm and determination to make it work. So I found a business partner, converted some nightclub owners into clients, and set up shop. With five hundred dollars in the bank, I incorporated my business, bartered for office space, and started invoicing for monthly retainers. My fear of not "making it" lit a fire under my ass to get my business off the ground—and fast.

I Was Somethin' Special

Now that I was an entrepreneur, *I had arrived.* Or so I thought. With this credential I had a new way of projecting myself onto the world: I was a twenty-one-year-old New York City entrepreneur representing the hottest nightclubs in town. My friends got off on the fact that all they had to do was say "Gabby" at the door to get access to all the hottest spots. I wore my title like a tattoo on my forehead. I thought I was pretty "special," and therefore better than most everyone.

My specialness led me to drop old friends and get totally hooked into the New York City "scene." Talk about illusion. This crowd was totally obsessed with the ego's projections. The scene was all about what we wore, what we did for a living, and who we knew. Those were the only details we cared about. No one even had a last name. It was Tommy the model, Jessica the door girl, or Mike the owner of [insert name of fancy company here]. This was all that mattered. Our egos projected our specialness onto one another to further our illusion that this world we'd created was real.

My need to feel special was not all that cool. Even though I'd found some way of perceiving myself on the outside, I still knew I was a fraud on the inside. I filled this hole with romantic relationships, binge eating, gossip, shopping, and the party scene. I stopped caring about my family and friends and instead became obsessed with the celebrity I'd brushed shoulders with the night before and being on the list at the latest new club. To make matters worse, my oh-so-special career was actually based on this crap. My business was promoting nightclubs.

Brief Encounters with Love

In the midst of this outside hustle, I could still hear my ~*ing* whisper from time to time. This whisper guided me to empower other young people with my career chutzpah. As a young entrepreneur, I'd been asked to speak at local universities on the topic of starting a business. Whenever I'd speak, I'd feel a rush of love come over me. I never needed to prepare my talks. It was as if someone were speaking through me. I flowed. After every lecture the young women in the room swarmed me. They were totally psyched to see someone their age out in the world, "making it." Little did they know I'd been out drinking till 4:00 a.m. But regardless of how hungover I may have been, something shone through me each time I lectured.

Around that time I was introduced to another young entrepreneur for business-to-business purposes. We'd meet weekly and brainstorm on how we could collaborate. Then one afternoon we started talking about all the amazing women we knew who had their own businesses. We agreed that they all needed some help promoting their ventures, and we decided to help them. In that one conversation we conceived the vision of the Women's Entrepreneurial Network (WEN), a network for women to connect and help further their endeavors. We immediately organized a networking event for all the female entrepreneurs in our Rolodexes. Three hundred women showed up.

WEN was a hit! It was too bad that the other areas of my life weren't flowing as freely as my speaking engagements and WEN events. Each day my business partnership grew more abusive, my addiction to the party scene intensified, and my need to be in a relationship amplified. I was on an endless search to feel good enough. And my ego had convinced me that everything I needed in order to feel complete was "out there." So I kept looking.

Shifting the Projector

After a few years in the New York City scene, my addiction to special romantic relationships began to dwindle as I became more obsessed with the special relationship with myself. I worked hard to convince myself that I didn't need a romantic partner to feel complete. This codependency began to look weak to my ego. I convinced myself that I was so kick-ass that I didn't need men as crutches anymore.

As soon as I made the commitment to be single, I transferred my addiction. I turned to my other love: partying. I put down the man and picked up the bash. This was an easy move for my ego. Once again I turned to something on the outside to complete me, and I found this completion in the nightlife scene. This was my home now, and the nameless faces in the club became my family.

Then I made a deal with the devil. My "casual" cocaine habit quickly morphed into a nightly routine. I didn't realize it while it was happening, but I was dying a slow death. I was hooked. The high I'd get from coke gave me everything I needed to stay out late and go home single. I lost my sex drive, my real friends, and more than twenty pounds. All the people I hung around with at this point were cokeheads. We were one and the same. I remember thinking, *Everyone does drugs.* Everyone I saw, anyway.

Hooked into the drugs as I was, there was still a whisper in the back of my mind reminding me of something better. I remember walking up to certain strangers in the nightclubs saying things like "You're good. And good knows good." I'm not sure whether this was prophetic or pathetic. I'd wax philosophical at after-parties, telling strangers about my plans to be a motivational speaker and self-help book author. I quoted the books I'd been trying to read and I proclaimed myself "super spiritual." I had no effing clue what spirituality meant, but there was something cool about perceiving myself that way.

Things spun out of control. Day turned into night and night turned into day. There was no weekend in my world. I was the girl out at the club on a Sunday wondering where the party was. I remember waking up to the clashing sounds of garbage trucks in the midst of a nasty hangover after two hours of sleep. My addiction got dark really fast. Every morning around 5:00 or 6:00 a.m., I'd return home from hours of partying. As I was walking home, people were leaving for work. I remember walking past the subway seeing people going to their offices. I was going nowhere.

Coming down was the worst. I'd do whatever I could to come down without too much depression. I'd pop some kind of downer, like Klonopin (a prescription anti-anxiety drug) or whatever drug I could convince the doctor to give me. I'd write in my journal until I fell asleep. In each entry I'd write about how I needed to stop using drugs and clean up. But then I'd fall off the wagon later that night. My life was a nightmare and I couldn't wake up. I couldn't wake up because I was unwilling to ask for help.

Things got really bad. I had no real friends, my family was constantly disappointed in me, I weighed about ninety-eight pounds, and my voice was totally shot. My business was going under, my business partner wanted me dead, and my self-loathing was at an all-time high. I was severely depressed from the drugs, and I literally had lost my mind. I couldn't remember where I'd parked my car the night before, or the name of the intern I'd hired a year earlier. I was a mess.

I Heard a Voice

My friends unsuccessfully attempted an intervention. It didn't work because though they weren't as bad as I was, they, too, were into drugs. I couldn't take them seriously. Then one night after a balls-out party I went home to try to come down and write in my journal. I remember writing, "I need help. God, Universe, whoever is out there . . . I surrender." Then I fell asleep. The next morning, October 2, 2005, I woke up to a loud inner voice. The whisper I'd been hearing for years was now a piercing call. The voice said, *Get clean and you'll have everything you want.* I was overwhelmed by this quick response to my cry for help. I had no other choice but to listen to the voice. It was clear that this was the answer.

Hear~*ing*

The voice I heard that morning is what the *Course* refers to as the Holy Spirit or Internal Teacher. I call it ~*ing* (inner guide or spirit). Our ~*ing*, as the *Course* defines it, is the intermediary between the fearful world of the ego and the loving mindset with which we came. The sole purpose of our ~*ing* is to guide our thoughts back to love. It is said in the *Course* that the moment we chose the tiny mad idea and separated from love, the spirit was placed inside our sleeping mind as a "call to awaken." The voice of our *~ing* dwells in what the *Course* refers to as our "right mind," and the primary function of this inner guide is to undo the ego's separation and guide our mind back to love.

Our *~ing* is always guiding us to use the world we see as a teaching device for reconditioning our fearful mind back to love. Our *~ing* is aware of all the pain, guilt, and fear we experience, yet knows none of it is real. When we turn to our *~ing* for help, we will always be guided out of the ego's illusions and into reality. Teaching us "true perception," the *~ing* guides us to replace our ego perceptions with love when we are ready to let those perceptions go. Our *~ing* does not judge our process and is patient as we're guided to learn. Our *~ing* is like a teacher who never gives up on us.

Our *~ing* is always on; we just forget to listen. As we become faithful to the ego, we deny the voice of our *~ing*.

Hitting Bottom to Hear

Often we need to hit a hard enough bottom to actually listen to the voice of our *~ing*. In my case I was so wrapped up in the ego's projections of the world that I was unable to truly hear the call for love inside me. I had to hit my knees and surrender in order to hear. This moment of surrender is what allows the voice to come through. It says in the *Course*, "*Trust not your good intentions. They are not enough. But trust implicitly your willingness, whatever else may enter.*"

It took a lot for me to surrender to my ~*ing*. I had to be a strung-out junkie to surrender and receive guidance. I'd hit rock bottom. Hitting bottom is actually a miracle because it creates a situation in which you are out of options and must ask for help. All the bottoms I've hit throughout my life collectively have been the catalyst for my greatest change. This bottom was my hardest, but in retrospect it was worth it. I had to fall apart to be willing to surrender to help and welcome in the voice of my ~*ing*.

I listened to that voice and have been sober since that day. The voice that intervened that morning was the voice of my inner guide. This was the whisper that had been with me for years, reminding me of a better way. I'd denied this distant whisper until I had no other choice. Hitting bottom and surrendering was the best thing that ever happened to me. It cracked me open and led me to hear the voice of my ~*ing* again. The willingness to hear this voice was all I needed to receive the guidance. The *Course* teaches that with the slightest willingness you will receive guidance from your inner guide. Our relationship with our ~*ing* is like having a mentor or a teacher. The ~*ing*'s sole purpose is to guide our thoughts back to love. Listening to the voice of your ~*ing* is central to the teachings of *A Course in Miracles*. Asking your ~*ing* for help is crucial.

My clients often get tripped up about the concept of communicating with their ~*ing*. They've become so accustomed to letting the voice of the ego run the show that welcoming in a voice of love seems difficult and somewhat confusing. In fact it's quite the opposite. Establishing a relationship with your ~*ing* is meant to be simple. All you have to do is ask. A gentle surrender to the love that lives within you is all you need. I've laid out some key tools for opening your heart and mind to igniting your relationship with your inner guide.

Three Steps to Turning Your Will over to Your ~*ing*

STEP 1. GENTLY SURRENDER

You can't force the voice of your ~*ing* to come forth. It's important to realize that the loving guidance has always been inside you, so you don't have to fight to find it. You just need to slow down and surrender. You may have felt a connection to your ~*ing* while in savasana at the end of a yoga class, walking on the beach, or through meditation. What's happened in these situations is that you've slowed your mind down enough to hear the voice of your inner guide. Hearing your ~*ing* requires a gentle surrender.

This surrender is often thrust upon us, as in my case

when I heard the voice guide me to get sober. I had hit such a hard bottom that I had no choice but to surrender to another inner voice. As hard as that bottom was, my surrender was gentle. I released my will to the care of something greater that night when I wrote in my journal. I asked for help.

Regardless of whether you've hit a hard bottom or just want to change, I'm sure you're ready to receive loving help. Why not? All you need is to be open to the possibility of guidance and surrender.

STEP 2. ASK FOR HELP

There is a big difference between wanting help and asking for it. Your ~*ing* is always with you and always guiding you, whether you listen or not. But once you're willing to hear the guidance, the next step is to ask for it. The act of asking for help deepens your surrender and awakens the voice of your ~*ing*. Your ~*ing* loves to be called on.

There are many ways to ask. Some powerful ways to call on your ~*ing* are through prayer, journaling, and internal dialogue.

■ *Prayer.* There is a prayer from the *Course* that I say each morning. It invites my ~*ing* to enter into my day and take the lead. The prayer is, *"Where*

90

would you have me go? What would you have me do? What would you have me say? And to whom?" This is a powerful way to begin your communication with your ~*ing*. This prayer surrenders your will over to the care of your ~*ing*, allowing the guidance to come forward.

- *Journaling.* My first correspondence with my ~*ing* unconsciously came through in my journal the evening of October 1, 2005, the night before I got sober. The moment I wrote "I need help. God, Universe, whoever is out there . . . I surrender," I was speaking to my ~*ing*. Feel free to ask your ~*ing* for help through your writing. Trust me, you're being heard.

- *Internal dialogue.* When I first began to invite my ~*ing* into my life, I would connect through my internal dialogue. As I struggled with my sobriety, forgiveness, and fear, I'd internally ask my ~*ing* for help. This was like a silent prayer. Each time I'd ask for help through my mind, I'd receive a loving response of some kind. Sometimes my anxiety would lift just knowing that I'd surrendered my problem. Other times I'd literally hear my ~*ing* speak back. By simply asking for help in my mind, I would receive the guidance.

STEP 3. WAIT PATIENTLY FOR A RESPONSE

The final step in asking your ~*ing* for help is to wait patiently for a response. Treat your ~*ing* like a mentor you really respect. Know that the response you will receive will have a profound impact. Therefore, be willing to wait patiently—it's worth it. Most likely you'll receive a response quickly, and it can come in many different ways. Some typical ways you'll hear the guidance are outlined below.

- *Intuition.* We'll often hear our ~*ing* as an intuitive feeling that comes over us. We'll feel as though we just know what direction to take. This intuition will not be based on fear; rather, it will come through as calm and peaceful. Our intuition will guide us to feel a certain way, to know something as truth, or to take certain action.

- *An inner voice.* Throughout the first few chapters I've been referring to this inner voice I kept hearing. You may think I'm a total nutbag, but I ask that you keep an open mind. When we hear the "voice" of our ~*ing*, it is almost like we're reading a book. You know how when you're reading, it's almost like you're hearing the voice of the narrator come through the page? That's what our *~ing* sounds like. It's an inner dialogue.

- *An external message.* Often our *~ing* will bring us messages and guide us to certain circumstances to help resolve an issue. When I first began paying attention to my inner guidance system, I started to pick up on some super cool coincidences. For instance, whenever I'd ask my *~ing* for help with an issue around my addiction recovery, I'd receive a phone call from a friend in my recovery program. It was like clockwork. It felt as though my inner guide had sent out a media alert that I needed help and my friends picked it up on the universal wire. These calls would come in almost instantaneously, and my friends would be there to help me work through whatever was coming up. My *~ing* was working through others to help restore my thoughts back to love.

Connecting to our inner guide is very simple. All we have to do is surrender, ask, and patiently wait for a response. Begin your practice when you feel moved to surrender. Know that by simply picking up this book you've already surrendered to the guidance of your *~ing*.

As we move into the next chapter you'll learn the most powerful tool for deepening your connection to your *~ing*.

Chapter 5 focuses on the miracle of forgiveness. Forgiveness releases us from the ego's stronghold and reignites our faith in love. Through the tools in the upcoming chapter you'll learn new ways to let go of your ego's projections and deepen your connection to spirit's truth. The exercises thus far have led you to see your ego in action. Recognizing the illusions you've created in your own mind will help you see your part in all situations and therefore support your forgiveness practice. Forgiveness helps us transcend our ego's fear and reconnect with our inner peace.

PART 2
The Answer

The F Word

Do you want a quietness that cannot be
disturbed, a gentleness that never can be hurt,
a deep abiding comfort, and a rest so perfect
it can never be upset? . . . All this forgiveness
offers you, and more.

—A COURSE IN MIRACLES

inety days into my sobriety, I could see more clearly. Three months of detox, sleep, coffee, and recovery meetings really did me good. One day at a time I stayed clean and rebuilt my life. I was showing up for myself big-time.

My recovery program emphasized forgiveness. There is a collective understanding within the sober community that serenity is a must-have and forgiveness is nonnegotiable. The core belief system is based on surrender and detachment from our old ways of being. This group and these principles offered a powerful bridge back to life.

One of their primary suggestions was to get on my knees and pray. I had no idea to whom or what I was praying, and I felt totally odd getting on my knees. *But I wanted what they had, so I did what they did.* I got on my knees every morning and every night and recited their suggested prayer. At first this ritual felt awkward, but with time I grew to like it. I felt I was making a commitment while connecting to a power greater than myself. I began to feel a lot physically while praying. At times I literally felt as though someone were standing above me, gently pressing me down as I prayed. I took this as a sign that I needed to stay down and keep praying.

Praying for myself became a daily practice. I asked for guidance, serenity, and peace. I asked for another day clean. This was difficult at first because I was so angry at myself for how I'd treated my body, my family, and my friends. I had a lot of cleanup to do. The people in my recovery program guided me to take a fearless inventory of my actions and recognize my shortcomings. Then they led me to release them to a higher power, aka God. The terminology behind this recovery work was new to me, but I was open to it nonetheless. Though I had no relationship with this "God," I was open and willing to learn. My recovery program reinforced that we could create a "God of our own understanding." This theory was much easier for me to wrap my head around. I always intuitively felt that there was something out there looking after me—a greater power. For years I'd felt this presence, but had no idea how to define it or consciously connect to it. I was relieved to know that all the guidance, energy, and intuition I'd felt throughout my life wasn't crazy after all.

To create a deeper connection with this Higher Power, I was guided to strengthen my practice of self-love and forgiveness. A major step in this process was to boldly assess my negative patterns. This process was profound for me. By taking this inventory I came to understand that fear was a common cause of most of my issues. Fear of being alone, fear of not being good enough, fear of getting too fat, fear of not having enough—the list goes on. Fear sat in the director's chair, calling the shots. Once I understood that fear had been in control, it was easier for me to forgive my past. I was able to honor myself for doing the best I could with an ego that had taken over my mind like a virus. I knew now that I had a disease in my mind. By praying for the release of these defects I was able to slowly begin to let go of the anger I felt toward myself. I was able to see myself with love for the first time in a long time.

My Dark Fantasy

When you first get clean, you're likely to experience a "pink cloud" period—you're super psyched to feel healthy and clear-headed. This was the case for me. Life began to flow and things got way better. Then, out of nowhere, my pink cloud turned gray. As soon as my ego got word that I was happy, it reached into its bag of tricks and took me down fast. Just because I was clean didn't mean I'd kicked my ego's patterns. The ego had a lot to latch on to, as I still was undergoing residual backlash. I was *feeling* for the first time in years, and therefore a whole bunch of shit was dredged up—everything I'd been numbing with the drugs. Even though I was praying every day and working on forgiveness, I still felt a tremendous amount of guilt, anger, and sadness over the wreckage from my past. The guilt I felt was the perfect tool for the ego to hook me into the illusion that the world was out to get me, and that I was unworthy of love.

To make matters worse, my ego created a whole new projection of specialness. I thought I was super special for being sober. I thought I was better than all the people I'd been partying with, better than my old friends, better than my business partner, and way better than anyone who needed drugs and alcohol to have a good time. This was a new kind of special that hooked me back into the ego's illusion of separation.

The Wall

For many people in early sobriety, the act of getting out of bed is an accomplishment. In my case I had no choice but to get out of bed to keep my PR company alive. My drinking and drugging hadn't done much for my business partnership, and it sure as hell hadn't done much for our bank account. So, in the midst of my personal recovery, I was rebuilding a business. Because I'd been such a hot mess for the majority of our professional relationship, my partner didn't have much reason to believe in me—even if

I was ninety days sober. Her resentment was strong and she wasn't ready to let it go. I know in her heart she was proud of me, but she wasn't willing to forget.

This drove me crazy. I felt as though I was constantly under a microscope. Not to mention I felt terrible if I ever needed to change a plan or come in late. This was the ego's way of keeping me stuck in the past. My ego had convinced me that not showing up on time or changing plans was horrific because it was something I used to do when I was hungover. Now when I had a legitimate reason to change plans or come in late, my ego would go nuts, making me feel terribly guilty. This was the perfect example of the ego taking a past experience and replaying it in the present moment. As a result, I was always on the defensive.

I brought up this issue in my recovery meetings. Week after week I'd bitch and moan about my resentment toward my business partner. But rather than join my hate parade, my friends in recovery guided me to see my part in the problem. They helped me see how I was perpetuating the dynamic by defending my current actions and projecting my own guilt onto her. They suggested I continue to pray to fully forgive myself. This I was willing to do. Then they suggested I pray for her. This confused me. *Why should I pray for her?* I thought. *I am the victim of drug addiction and I am the special one getting sober.* They encouraged me to get over myself and take their suggestion. They asked me to pray for her to have all the peace and happiness I wanted for myself. Most important, they suggested I be willing to forgive her.

They taught me that by defending myself I was making things worse. There is a lesson in the *Course* that reinforces this concept: *"In my defenselessness my safety lies."* By defending against her anger toward me, I was reinforcing the illusion. My defense was adding fuel to the fire and reiterating that I'd done something wrong. By choosing defenselessness instead, I could stay in the present moment rather than dig up the past. This was hard at first, but I was willing.

Release

Despite my willingness, I still hadn't officially thrown down the *F* word and forgiven her. I was toying with the idea, but had trouble committing. Then that winter I took a ski trip out west with a friend. Her flight back home left before mine, and mine got canceled due to a snowstorm. I was left behind and psyched to have another day to ski. I woke up the next morning and was the first person on the chair lift. As I traveled up the lift I looked to the right and to the left, and all I could see were snow-capped mountains and a clear blue sky. I gazed down at the mountain covered in powder, thrilled that mine would be the first skis to hit the snow. I was in heaven.

Then, like clockwork, an ego thought burst my love bubble. I immediately started obsessing about having to face my partner the next day in the office. I got hooked into the idea that she'd be mad at me for coming back a day late even though I was snowed in. This ego tornado was about to rip through the peace of my snow day.

Then I experienced a divine intervention. I heard an inner voice say, *Forgive her.* These odd voices and moments of peace were becoming the norm. I was getting used to hearing this inner voice, and I was now fully willing to listen. So I took the suggestion from my inner guide and I said a prayer. I prayed for her to have all the peace and happiness that I wanted for myself. Then, in an instant, something lifted. I immediately felt lighter and more serene. I could see my surroundings more clearly and I could breathe more freely. I released my anger and forgave. Free from my resentment, I felt my skis hit the powder and I flew down the mountain, unburdened and exhilarated.

My Dark Fantasy Turns to Light

From that day forward our relationship was never the same. I was a big step closer to knowing the miracle of forgiveness. I learned that forgiveness isn't just about letting the other person off the hook—it's about releasing ourselves. When I forgave her I set myself free from the bonds of the ego. The ego had convinced me that I was separate from her and that I was the victim. This perception that I was a victim led me to attack her in order to protect myself. It also led me to defend against her illusion, thereby reinforcing it. This is a vicious cycle. The darkness I saw in her was a reflection of the darkness I believed to be true in myself. Sure, it seemed as though I'd been harmed and that I couldn't possibly forget. But holding on kept me connected to the projection of being the victim, making me feel like crap on a daily basis. I'd wake up each day to rehearse the role of victim.

The only way out for me was through forgiveness. By choosing to forgive and perceive her with love, I released myself from the ego's story. I realize now that I wasn't mad at her; I was mad at myself for believing in the projection of hatred that we'd created. I knew in my heart that only love was real, and that she was just projecting her own fear onto me. I knew deep down that she wanted to see with love, too. I set myself free by choosing love over fear.

Not only did I feel relieved, but I noticed a massive shift in her energy. The day I got back, she didn't bother me about coming in late. In fact, she was happy to see me. Our dynamic had shifted because I had shifted. The outside world reflects our internal state, and when we shift our perceptions, the world shifts accordingly. The newfound light I saw in her was reflecting back at me.

Practicing the *F* Word

Forgiveness is totally awesome. When you connect to light within others, you can see them as equal and release your resentments. If the light in you reflects the light in them, you can choose to see only their light. It is your choice to forgive and release the darkness. It is your choice to see with love.

Forgiveness tears down the ego's walls of separation and reunites us as one. The anger and fear of the ego's illusion disappear. There's no more "he said, she said." It all just lifts. It feels as though chains have been removed and you've been set free from a lifetime of terror. Why continue rehearsing the role of victim when you could be free and happy?

Now is the time when I throw down "the *F* word" and start teaching you the *Course's* tools for forgiveness. I will break it down in four steps. While there are suggested steps, the process of forgiveness is unique to everyone. There is no specific time frame, and no need to rush the process.

The first step is to recognize how the ego has been attacking others. The second step is to know that the attack on others is merely an attack on you, and to become willing to release the illusion. Finally, you'll let your ~*ing* take the wheel and guide you to forgive. All you'll need for transformation is some willingness and your ~*ing*. Now let me break it down for you.

Breakin' Down the *F* Word

F WORD STEP 1. RECOGNIZE THE ILLUSION

"An unforgiving thought does many things. In frantic action it pursues its goal, twisting and overturning what it sees as interfering with its chosen path. Distortion is its purpose, and the means by which it would accomplish it as well. It sets about its furious attempts to smash reality, without concern for anything that would appear to pose a contradiction to its point of view."

This passage from the *Course* reinforces the destruction that occurs when we're unwilling to forgive. I spent four years letting this distorted way of thinking dominate my professional relationship. My willingness to see this differently and recognize my unforgiving thoughts launched the forgiveness process.

The first step toward forgiving my business partner was to recognize the illusion that my ego had created. I looked closely at the situation, and witnessed how I'd made myself the victim and made her wrong about everything. I'd decided to see only her anger and resentment and focus on her darkness. Upon looking more closely at the situation, I realized the darkness was not in her, but was an illusion I'd created in my mind and played on loop. I had two choices. I could choose to look at her darkness or to see her light. By choosing to look at her darkness, I was amplifying the darkness that existed in my mind.

Recognizing that this was my choice didn't mean I ignored her part in the situation. In fact, the *Course* says, *"This does not deny the darkened spots of sin in someone, but only that they are irrelevant to my perception."* I was able to acknowledge her negativity, but chose not to hook into it. Remember that you have a choice in what you see. If you choose to see a person's darkness, you strengthen your darkness within. If you choose to see their light, you shine from the inside out.

Once I genuinely understood that the darkness I chose to see in her was amplifying more darkness inside me, I was willing to release her. I saw my projection clearly and was open to release what the *Course* calls the "wall I had placed between us."

This is a challenging step. You'll realize what is taught in lesson 190 of the *Course*, which is that the gun you've been pointing at others you've actually been pointing at yourself. In other words, the guilt is not in the other person, but rather, as the *Course* says, "I *am the secret murderer.*"

Though this may not be comfortable, it is a crucial step. Simply look at the ways in which you've chosen to focus on the darkness rather than the light. Ask yourself, *How have I chosen to see darkness in this situation?*

F WORD STEP 2. RELEASE JUDGMENT

"Forgiveness, on the other hand, is still, and quietly does nothing. It offends no aspect of reality, nor seeks to twist it to appearances it likes. It merely looks, and waits, and judges not. He who would not forgive must judge, for he must justify his failure to forgive. But he who would forgive himself must learn to welcome truth exactly as it is."

This passage from the *Course* guides us to see how judgment reinforces our unwillingness to forgive. By judging my partner, I kept our unforgiving dynamic alive. Once I released my judgment against her, I was able to take a huge step toward forgiving her. Take this time to acknowledge how you've been judging those people you need to forgive. Ask yourself, *How have I been judging?*

F WORD STEP 3. BE WILLING TO FORGIVE

An awesome line from the *Course* reads, *"Do you prefer to be right or happy?"* It's far too often that the response is that we'd rather be right. Being "right" doesn't get us any-where. We can bend over backwards to reinforce the idea that we're victims, but that doesn't make us feel good. The willingness to release the need to be right is a major step toward forgiveness. This step will guide you to the happy fact that all you need to do is be willing to release the role of victim and choose to see something different.

As soon as I became willing to stop being right and start being happy, I was able to welcome in an opportunity to forgive. Without my willingness, I wouldn't have been led to forgive my partner that day on the ski lift.

Look closely at the choice you have made, and become willing to choose differently. Say out loud, "I am willing to release the wall that I have placed between us." Then sit in meditation and let me be your guide. You can use the writ-ten meditation below or download my guided meditation from www.gabbyb.tv/meditate.

F Word Meditation

Begin your meditation with this silent prayer:
"Inner guide, please lead me to know the truth.
Lead me to release all attack, fear, judgment, and
anger. Help me forgive.

I welcome forgiveness as my safety, serenity, and
inner peace.

I welcome happiness and release.

Thank you."

Sit up straight in your seat.

Take a deep breath in through your nose and let it
out through your mouth.

Continue this cyclical breath.

In your mind, invite in the image of someone you
have been resenting, possibly even yourself.

See this person standing before you.

Look them in the eye.

Breathe in: I am willing to forgive you.

Breathe out: I see the truth and the truth is only
love.

Breathe in: I choose to see the light in you.

Breathe out: The light I see in you is a reflection of
my inner light.

Breathe in: I choose to forgive.

F WORD STEP 4. ASK YOUR ~*ing* FOR HELP

"Do nothing, then, and let forgiveness show you what to do."

The final step is simple. The *Course* teaches that this step is not our responsibility.

Once you look at how the ego has kept the illusion alive, you see how you've chosen its dark fantasy. The *Course* suggests that you look at the darkness without judgment, and remember to laugh at the tiny mad idea of separation. When you do this, you can release this mistake to the care of your ~*ing*. Know that when you turn to your ~*ing* for help, you can release the illusion and be led to forgive.

Once I looked closely at the darkness I'd focused on in my relationship with my partner, I was able to see that it was my choice. Then, by releasing my judgment of her and becoming willing to forgive, I was prepared to turn to my ~*ing* for help. The final step was the easiest. I just prayed each day to let my ~*ing* intervene and set me free from my resentment. I didn't know how or when I'd forgive her, but I knew guidance was on the way. I remained patient, allowing my ~*ing* to take the lead.

Now let your ~*ing* step in. Ask for help and remain patient as your inner guide transforms your thoughts back to love, releasing the illusion for good. Begin a daily prayer practice of asking for help and releasing your resentment over to the care of your inner guide. Say out loud, "I choose to see this differently; thank you for guiding me to forgive." Then be patient. You cannot control when or how forgiveness will come. Just stay willing and open to forgiveness. Your ~*ing* will show up in many unique ways. For instance, I had no idea I was going to forgive my partner on a ski lift! There's no way I could have planned that.

Just stay willing and open about this process, and you'll learn that *"the secret walls of defense are no longer needed, and so have disappeared. In their place is the light of forgiveness, which shines the way to the home we never left. And thus it is no secret we are healed."* Forgiveness is the bedrock of the spiritual journey you have embarked on with me. Through forgiveness you can shine light on the darkness of the ego and find inner peace. In the next chapter the *F* word will come in handy. I will teach you how my *Course* work has taught me that all relationships are assignments. Through my dedication to forgiveness, I've been able to show up for these assignments with love and grow more spiritually connected. Take this powerful tool with you as we continue to add new layers to your journey back to love.

6

Relationships Are Assignments

No one is sent by accident to anyone.

—A COURSE IN MIRACLES

arly addiction recovery is like plugging the holes of a sinking ship: once you plug one hole, another one appears. This was the case for me. As soon as I put down the drugs and the alcohol, all my other addictions flooded back in. I turned to food, work, shopping, and relationships to avoid dealing with my ego's fear. Overeating was a great way for me to numb out at first. I'd plan each meal hours in advance for a sense of control. Then I'd binge to fill myself up. This pattern kept me focused on something other than my pain.

At first I just ate over my feelings, and then I began to date over them. When overeating no longer worked, I turned to my best avoidance tactic of all: romantic relationships. Sounds like a broken record, right? It is. The ego replays the same projections over and over to keep us from healing. Rather than focusing on inner growth, my ego convinced me to keep looking outside for serenity and peace. Though I was feeling much healthier, I was still hooked on the ego's illusion that I wasn't safe without a man. I jumped in and out of six-month relationships, with someone always waiting on the sidelines. My codependency followed me around like a sick dog. This was very shameful for me.

To make matters worse, I continued to repeat the same patterns in all my relationships. *Remember, the ego takes the fear from the past and projects it onto the present and the future.* These insecure patterns were based on my deep-rooted fear of someone leaving me alone. Therefore, I'd do whatever it took to keep the relationship going. This played out in some super-whacked-out ways. For instance, I tried to be cool by going along with whatever the guy liked—I was never my authentic self because I wanted to be what I thought they wanted. I denied my truth. Playing the role of "cool girl" never worked. Ironically, this behavior was the opposite of what men wanted. They wanted to be with a confident, authentic woman—not a girl trying to act cool.

My ego's pattern was to hold on to the relationship by manipulating someone to view me as cool so they wouldn't leave. This created a very nasty dynamic because though I was acting "cool" on the outside, I was a complete mess on the inside. My mind was in a constant frenzy, obsessing over when he'd call, when we'd get together, and what the future held for our relationship. My ego nailed me with the future-tripping. Within a week of entering a new relationship, I'd fast-forward to see myself walking down the aisle and celebrating our son's bar mitzvah. This future-tripping stemmed from my ego's belief that one "special" person would save me as soon as I had a ring on my finger. Even though I never voiced these thoughts, I know the energy behind them was apparent. No matter how cool I acted, I always gave off a vibe that I was needy, insecure, and incomplete without a man. This energy was totally vile; therefore, the relationships would always end. Worst of all, I felt terrible that I didn't have enough self-love to combat the ego's projections of special idols.

Sin and Guilt

Now that I was sober and committed to the lessons of the *Course*, I could witness the chaotic patterns I'd play out in my train-wreck romantic relationships. By this point in my recovery I was wise enough to recognize that I was caught in another ego pattern. This made me hate myself. I could see clearly how I'd turned my back on love and let the ego mindset take the wheel. Each day I spent stuck in my co-dependence disconnected me from spirituality. This decision to forget love and choose fear made me feel as though I'd done something wrong. This is what the *Course* refers to as "sin." Though I didn't realize it, deep down I felt I'd turned my back on my loving truth.

The inner belief that I had sinned drowned me in guilt, which came from the fact that my mind had joined with the wrong teacher, the ego. Each time I'd spin out in some addictive relationship pattern, I'd feel guilty about it, as though I'd killed the potential for happiness and self-love. Guilt is the feeling we experience as a response to the belief that we've sinned against love—it's a projection of the sadness we have for neglecting love. Whenever we choose the ego over ~ing, we subconsciously think we've sinned and therefore feel guilty. Think about it. If deep down we believed that only love was real, wouldn't we feel devastated if we dropped that love and picked up fear instead? Of course we would! That's why we feel so crappy when we choose the ego over love as our teacher. We think we've done something terrible, and we also think *we* are terrible. Unconsciously we believe we deserve punishment because we turned our back on love.

The involuntary feeling of having sinned against love really brought me down. Guilt arose from this sadness. This guilt was inevitable because deep down I knew that I was denying this awesome other way of being. Underneath all my codependent patterns was an inner cheerleader reminding me that I was independent and wonderful. Instead of listening to that voice of love and recognizing that the problem was in my mind, my ego instead focused on special romantic partners to keep the illusion alive.

Since we don't realize the problem is in our mind, we take that guilt and project it outward. This creates more guilt. Then we seek guilt in everyone and everything. Projecting guilt onto others is a really crafty trick. Each outward projection keeps us from recognizing that the problem is in our mind. If we don't recognize it in our mind, the ego can survive. Therefore the ego leads us to believe that we can relieve our guilt by attacking others and projecting sin onto them. For instance, whenever I felt guilty I blamed the outside world. I blamed my incompleteness on the guy who didn't like me, the client who ended the contract, or the friend who wasn't returning my calls. I did this rather than recognize that the only incomplete problem was my belief in incompleteness. The ego's "protection" of guilt actually creates more of it and we become unconsciously attracted to it.

Denial

To keep me from turning inward for help, the ego reached into its bag of tricks and pulled out denial. The ego denied love in order to keep me stuck in the darkness, convincing me that fear was my only source of safety. By denying love, the ego made fear my companion. Therefore I needed to hold on to these projections in order to function in the fearful world I'd accepted—once again the ego convinced me that all of the safety, security, and peace I was seeking was in the arms of a special partner.

To further deny the potential for love, my mind became more convinced of my inadequacy and unworthiness. I held on tightly to the stories I'd grown to believe in: "I can't be alone," "I'm not good enough for them," and so on. By digging up my inadequacy the ego hooked me back into idolizing my romantic partners and seeing myself as separate. By separating myself from these romantic partners I was denying my own greatness and perceiving them as better than I was. The ego's denial protected my belief in fear. Though things were getting better in most every area of my life, the ego held on to my fear in romantic relationships. It held on for dear life.

Feeling Like a Fraud

I lived for a while in this pseudo-recovery mode, still battling my codependency, in and out of the guilt cycle. Though the ego had cornered this one area of my life, I still grew tremendously in all others. I stayed sober and worked on my spiritual practice, prayed, forgave, and positively changed many aspects of my life. This work was so inspiring to me that I felt the desire to share it. My former lecture-circuit routine of speaking on panels and in classrooms about entrepreneurship and marketing had now shifted. At this point I was more interested in lecturing on happiness and recovery than on vocational topics. In addition, I had fully released my PR career and had begun supporting myself as a life coach and speaker.

My work was well received. I believed deeply in what I

was teaching, and my messages resonated with many young women. My lecture rooms grew from forty people to a hundred within a few months. The lecture halls looked like sample sales, only the women were searching for happiness rather than a discount on designer clothes. My coaching practice began to take off, and I was doing this work full-time.

I loved lecturing and coaching—but deep down I still felt guilty. Even though I'd made miraculous changes in my life, my ego was still in the driver's seat when it came to my romantic relationships. I was paralyzed by the fear of being alone or not being good enough for a romantic partner.

The guilt got worse when I started coaching young women on their relationship issues. I remember guiding one of my clients through a breakup. I taught her the *Course's* messages of how the ego makes romantic partners into idols and how the relationship was an assignment. In the midst of my lesson I felt overwhelmed with guilt. I knew in my gut that I was a fraud. I heard my ~*ing* say, *Get it together, girl! You need to teach this stuff. It's time to kick this fear once and for all!* This inner voice screamed loud enough for me to stop avoiding and surrender. I couldn't continue this cycle of replaying my ego's romantic fears only to feel guilty that I'd denied love, and I no longer felt satisfied by projecting this guilt onto others. I had to turn down the volume of my ego and release this limiting belief once and for all.

Willingness to See Relationships as Assignments

My willingness to change was all I needed. The *Course* had taught me, *"What is concealed cannot be loved, and so it must be feared."* I couldn't conceal my issues in relationships any longer. It was time to shine light on the problem and be willing to release the ego's stronghold.

With the slightest willingness I was guided. It so happened that my *Course* study at this time was focused on how relationships are assignments. *A Course in Miracles* tells us that all relationships are chosen by our ~*ing* for one purpose: to learn to see each other as love. The *Course* teaches, *"When you meet anyone, remember it is a holy encounter. As you see him, you will see yourself. As you treat him, you will treat yourself. As you think of him, you will think of yourself. Never forget this, for in him you will find yourself or lose yourself."* After reading this I could breathe again! In an instant it became clear to me that my romantic dramas were an opportunity for growth rather than a lifelong prison sentence. This part of the text taught me that I was guided to every relationship to transcend the ego's belief in separation, that if I welcomed each encounter as a holy encounter, I could learn to stop judging, fearing, attacking, and making others special, and instead see them as one. See them as myself. All I had to do was welcome the holy encounter. It was time to stop hiding from these awesome assignments and let the healing begin. So I committed to rip off the Band-Aid and let my ~*ing* do her thing.

I turned to the *Course* for further guidance on how I could show up for these so-called "holy encounters." I quickly learned that each relationship we enter into offers us two options: to show up as two separate people looking for completion in one another; or to show up as two whole people coming together to enjoy their wholeness. Now, I didn't know too many people I considered whole, and it became clear to me that I wasn't alone. We all had work to do! And if we waited until we were fully healed before we started a relationship, we'd put Match.com out of business. Therefore we have to recognize relationships as assignments that will bring all our neuroses to the table. When we show up for these assignments we can start dealing and begin healing. The *Course* positions relationships as one of the most significant opportunities for us to learn and grow. Through another person we can come to know ourselves.

When we're stuck in the ego's illusion, we believe that all our encounters with others are random and accidental. Before I could see my patterns I envisioned each romantic partner as someone I'd stumbled upon or met at a bar or through a friend. Now I understand that none of these relationships was accidental. The *Course* teaches the opposite: there are no chance encounters. When we perceive the relationship as an assignment, we can begin to see how our intentions have created perfect opportunities for either ego misery or transformational growth. If we're willing to grow spiritually and call on our *~ing* for help, we'll be guided to the perfect relationship assignment that will provide us with the best possible learning opportunities. If we're unwilling to grow, then we'll continue to play out the same crazy crap in all our relationships. The form of each relationship assignment is unique, but the goal is to come together to ignite the memory of love.

Now that I understood that relationships were assignments, I agreed to show up for whatever came my way. Since I was willing to change, I knew that I'd be guided to the perfect romantic partner. I was psyched for my next relationship because it was time to get to work. However, my idea of the perfect partner was much different from what the Universe had in store for me. I thought I'd be guided to a nice guy with whom I could share and openly work through my issues. What I really needed was the exact opposite. If I were truly willing to release my pattern and show up for the assignment, then I'd be guided to the "perfect guy" who'd dig up all my shit so that I'd have to surrender to and choose love over fear. And that's what I got.

Mr. Big Assignment

Once again I called in the same type of relationship that I'd been attracting for over a decade. He was handsome, smart, artistic, cool, and totally unavailable. I feared this at first, but deep down I accepted it as my assignment. This guy was perfect because he'd bring up all my issues around not feeling worthy without male attention. Had I entered into a relationship with a guy who doted on me, I wouldn't have had a chance to grow.

Each day in this relationship was a struggle. My deep desire to feel complete on my own battled with my horrifying need to be saved. This inner turmoil went on for several months. I acted out in all the old ego ways by attacking myself, attacking him in my mind, and fueling my fear of abandonment with my ego's crazy mind games. None of the ego's stories were real, but neither was the relationship. What I wanted out of it was not what I was receiving. This brought up all of my issues. I felt inadequate and less-than. I made him super special and idolized him like crazy. I held on tightly to this relationship and did everything I could to seem cool in his eyes.

In the midst of all this old behavior, I knew there was a better way and I was still willing to accept it. I wasn't sure how I'd fully release my ego in this area, but I did the best I could to cope. It wasn't that he was a mean guy; he just wasn't that available. He was super into my professional success . . . and other than that, pretty into himself. I was crumbling on the inside, wishing he would want what I wanted and manipulating him with ass-kissing and a "cool girl" attitude. This was manipulation because it wasn't my truth. I acted like this to try to make him stay.

After a year in this unfulfilling relationship I had to find solace. I'd spent my nights crying and my days paralyzed by the fear of losing him. I was desperate for relief. I'd hit bottom, and it was time to ask for help. So, rather than continue jumping through hoops for his attention, I hit my knees and started praying.

~*ing*Tervention

It's funny how willing I was to surrender certain issues to my ~*ing*, whereas I let my ego run the show with my relationships. This area of my life was the ego's stomping ground in my mind, and surrendering was an incredible challenge. But I was no longer willing to stay chained to the ego. There were no more quick solutions to this problem. No "five steps to getting a man" or "six steps to 'I do.'" None of that worked. My only option was to put down the practical and pick up the spiritual. The *Course* taught me that I couldn't recover from the ego on my own. I needed an ~*ing*Tervention. My *Course* work had taught me that when you welcome the Holy Spirit (~*ing*) in for guidance, you will receive. The *Course* says, *"The Holy Spirit always sides with you and with your strength. As long as you avoid His guidance in any way, you want to be weak."* I had to side with the strength of something greater than myself. Once again, I turned to my ~*ing* for help.

My ~ing had hooked me up every time before, so I followed the Course's suggestion to invite in my inner guide for help. I got on my knees each morning and night. I kept asking for help. I still wasn't clear about whom I was talking to, but I pretended it was a big sister or a friend. I'd say, "Inner guide, I need a hook-up here. Once again I'm obsessing over a guy and I am ready to release this cycle. Show me what you've got!"

Though I didn't feel immediate relief, I noticed many moments of guidance. For instance, a friend invited me to a lecture that provided me with great spiritual tools for releasing romantic illusions. I also continually heard about books that were powerful for overcoming codependency and love addiction. Then I was guided to a women's group that came together to support one another's codependent patterns. Whether I knew it or not, I was being guided. I replayed Marianne Williamson's audio lecture *The Language of Letting Go* over and over like a Top 40 hit. She cited the Course's messages on forgiveness and release, and reminded me to welcome the assignment and remain willing to change.

Letting Spirit Take the Wheel

I began to see my ~ing get to work. All the guidance I was receiving was tremendously helpful. I relished my meditation, Marianne's audio, and my recovery groups. I experienced many moments of relief and began to feel taken care of. I was still acting out with my ego in romantic relationships, but I was making progress. I accepted progress rather than perfection and I stayed down on my knees in prayer.

The *Course* teaches that prayer is the medium of miracles. When we pray for our *~ing* to help, we welcome a new perception. In our prayer we release our control and stop trying to manage every detail of our lives. I felt this deeply. When I prayed I allowed a power greater than myself to take control. I welcomed in guidance, I welcomed in a shift in perception, and I created a miracle. In this case the miracle was that I began to feel better and allowed my *~ing* to lead me to heal.

Welcome Your Own *~ing*Tervention

The purpose of this chapter is to help you begin to see your relationships as assignments. Once again we'll follow the *Course* and keep it simple. Rather than try to figure out each issue and find a solution, you'll just turn to your *~ing* for help. Allow an *~ing*Tervention to occur and let spirit lead you to see what you need to learn from all relationships. My willingness to let spirit lead me is what enabled me to show up for my relationship assignments and stop denying my fear. The fact that I'd called on my *~ing* for help is what allowed me to hear it fully. Our *~ing* is guiding us all the time, but if we're not open to receiving, we'll miss the guidance. Therefore, this chapter is an opportunity to bring your ~ing into your relationships. As the *Course* teaches, *"It is only in relationships that salvation can be found."* Allow the following steps to guide you as you begin to see your relationships as opportunities to heal. These exercises will shine light on the dark illusions the ego has created in relationships. You, too, can experience miraculous guidance as soon as you stop manipulating and start praying.

Be Willing to See the Assignments

We can apply the following steps to all relationships in our life. We begin by welcoming in the assignment. If we're unwilling to receive the assignment, we'll continue to bulldoze past it and stay stuck in the illusion. That's no fun. Remember, the ego's illusion in relationships kicks up all its nasty tricks. In all ego-driven relationships you will attack, judge, and make separate and special. The ego goes to town when other people are involved. Once we understand that each encounter is an assignment, we begin to illuminate the ego's tricks.

Look at the Problem as It Is

Witness how the ego has set up your relationships. Whenever we perceive a problem we project it outward, typically onto others. We start to tell ourselves, *The problem's not in me, it's in someone else.* This lesson will help you see that all our suffering comes from a belief in our mind—a wrong-minded choice to believe in fear. The *Course* suggests, "*No one can escape from illusions unless he looks at them. For not looking is the way they are protected.*" Rather than shrink from the illusions of the ego and avoid the problem, we can simply look at it. When we acknowledge that we created the problem in our mind, we can see how the ego interfered. This is when suffering ends. The moment we recognize that we've chosen incorrectly, we can choose the right teacher. That is the miracle. In my case, I recognized that I was stuck in the ego's guilt cycle by teaching others to be fearless when I was stuck in fear—and that moment led me to ask for a miracle. The miracle helps us recognize that we've chosen to believe in the nasty world of the ego, and that it is not real. The miracle occurs when we remember that fear is not real. We have chosen to dream the dreams of separation and guilt so that we remain asleep in the ego's nightmare.

If we truly want to end our suffering, we must recognize that *we* put it there and that we chose it in our mind. When we recognize that what we've experienced is of the ego, we can then invite spirit in. Spirit can enter into our mind to heal the ego's projections, reminding us that we are all one. Suffering and sickness come directly from the feeling of separation. The healing comes from realizing that we are not separate from anyone.

This exercise is designed to help you see that your problems are not external to you, but instead are in your mind. Most of this work is about truly realizing how we've grown to trust the ego over love. Each time we look at the ego directly, we come closer to knowing it is not real. Take your time with this exercise. Each time you witness yourself projecting fear onto others or blaming a relationship for your problems, gently remind yourself, *The problem is not in them, it's in my mind.* Acknowledging this truth will guide you to become willing to welcome an ~*ing*Tervention.

Welcome an ~*ing*Tervention

Begin your work with a practice of reviewing your relationships. Look closely at how the ego has played a role in each one. Ask yourself, *What is my assignment?* and then sit in meditation for five minutes and let your ~*ing* respond. For additional guidance you can download my "Meditation on Relationships" from www.gabbyb.tv/meditate. Allow my voice to guide you as you welcome in your ~ing for guidance.

Meditation on Relationships

In silent meditation we welcome in guidance to see all our relationships as holy.

Sit up straight in your chair with your feet planted firmly on the ground.

Gently breathe in through your nose and out through your mouth.

Identify your most challenging relationship.

Invite your inner guide to remind you of your interconnectedness.

Breathe in: ~ing, help me see love in this relationship.

Breathe out: I welcome this assignment.

Breathe in: Thank you for helping me change my mind about my wrong projections.

Breathe out: Thank you for reminding me of what is real.

I welcome in the holy encounter where I can see this person as my equal. Where we are both love.

~ing-Write

Immediately following your meditation, pick up your pen and ~ing-write (freewrite) for ten minutes. The topic of the ~ing-write is "How have I projected my fear onto others?" Let your pen flow and allow your ~ing to guide you to understand your assignment.

Show Up

It's one thing to recognize the assignment, but it's another thing entirely to show up for it. Remember that showing up for the assignment is one of the most powerful ways to restore your thoughts back to love. By seeing love in the face of another person you know the true meaning of oneness. Allow all your resentments to become assignments and show up for them one day at a time.

Know that you'll receive all the support you need along the way. Keep in mind that your ~ing works through people; as the Course says, "No one is sent by accident to anyone." Pay attention to those who are there to serve your growth. Listen and be guided.

In the coming chapter you'll deepen your understanding of the holy encounter. Take your work from this chapter with you as I guide you to deepen your faith in miracles. By committing to the work, you will learn to rely on your ~*ing* rather than on your ego. As you start to feel the relief of choosing love over fear, you'll come to wonder why you ever chose otherwise.

7

The Holy Instant

The holiest of all the spots on earth is where an
ancient hatred has become a present love.

—A COURSE IN MIRACLES

* ◆ *

sking my ~*ing* for help became a daily habit. This prac-tice of constant contact with spirit activated the guid-ance around me. By consciously asking my ~*ing* for help, I experienced tons of synchronicity. People I needed to con-nect with would call out of the blue, books I needed to read fell off the shelf, and I felt a strong overall sense of connection to the Universe. I didn't perceive any of this as coincidence or dumb luck, but rather as frequent messages from my inner guide.

Then the synchronicity became even groovier. One of my neighbors suggested I set up a business-to-business meeting with a woman named Rha Goddess, who, like me, worked to empower young women. A week later, an-other friend independently suggested I meet Rha Goddess. These back-to-back referrals were enough for me to accept the Universal memo and e-mail her to schedule a meet-ing. She responded to my e-mail by saying that she couldn't meet right away because she'd be out of the country visiting a spiritual healer in Brazil. I was shocked: I, too, was going to be visiting the same spiritual healer, the same week as

Rha. I flipped out over this synchronicity, but it didn't seem to faze her.

Though there weren't many people at the spiritual grounds in Brazil, we never did meet there. On the flight home, I connected to the woman sitting next to me on the plane. I told her what I did for work and that I lived in New York City. She replied, "You must meet this woman." She then handed me the business card of Rha Goddess. I laughed as the Universe hit me over the head yet again. One week after I got back from Brazil, I traveled to New Orleans for Eve Ensler's V-Day event (a global activist movement to stop violence against women and girls). When I got there, I looked over the line up of performers and speakers for the first day. Rosario Dawson was speaking on the main stage at noon, followed by Jane Fonda at one o'clock and then, at two, a poetry performance by guess who? Rha Goddess! Clearly I needed to meet this woman. The guidance was so apparent that I felt overwhelmed with joy. I loved this magnificent synchronicity because it reinforced my faith that I was being guided. I was able to see clearly how my ~ing was leading me to Rha for some important reason.

Finally we met. After her performance, we gave each other a big hug and laughed about how a power greater than ourselves was working hard to get us together. We agreed to set up our long-awaited meeting later that month.

We decided to meet for dinner in Brooklyn. The dark, rainy day mirrored my state of mind. As usual, I was tripped up about my romantic relationship. Even though I'd been showing up for the assignment and taking many fearless actions, I was still trapped by the ego with the fear of being alone, not being good enough, and feeling incomplete. In an effort to release some of this fear, I spent the entire day meditating.

Finally I pulled myself together and drove to Brooklyn to meet with Rha. The moment we sat down, we began talking about our personal lives rather than business. Remember, we didn't know anything about each other except for what we could glean from a few Google searches. She told me about her spiritual beliefs and her coaching practice. She also told me about her magnificent husband and how she had manifested the relationship. She explained how she got over her negative relationship patterns and became clear about what she wanted in order to free up space to call in her man. She exuded light when she spoke about her husband and their relationship. Then I heard my ~*ing* speak loudly: *Ask her to be your coach!* I listened to my ~*ing* and said, "Do you still coach people?" She responded, "In fact, I do. Each year I coach a handful of people who are already deep into their spiritual journey. My work is to take them to the next level. I coach people just like you."

From that day forward Rha was my coach. It was clear to me that my call for help was answered. Spirit works through people. When we ask our ~*ing* for help, often it comes in the form of another human being. Many times these people we're guided to will turn out to be our greatest teachers. In this case my *~ing* was leading me to meet the perfect guide for releasing my romantic illusions.

Showing Up for the Assignment

When the student is ready, the teacher appears. I was ready to get to work. Rha and I agreed that releasing my romantic illusions topped my list of things to work on, and she put me on a six-month plan of facing those demands. She helped me become even clearer about how I was limited by my belief that I was incomplete without a man. She helped me feel past wounds and honor all of my feelings as equally important. Then she guided me to become honest and unapologetic about what I wanted in a romantic partner. Finally she helped me realize how my current relationship had taught me everything I could learn at that time, and that it was no longer serving me. All this work, combined with my *Course* studies, led me to create some miraculous shifts.

Patiently Receiving Guidance

Within six months of working with Rha, I had more clarity than ever before. For the first time in my life I was unapologetic about what I wanted in a romantic relationship.

It was clear that my desires did not match up to my current relationship. At first this revelation really kicked my ego into high gear. I judged my boyfriend for not being able to give me what I wanted, and my mind went into attack mode. However, this type of ego thinking no longer resonated with me. I had shone a lot of light on this dark area of my life, and through my *Course* work and Rha's coaching I was able to choose not to judge and attack. Rather than go all psycho on him, I decided to throw down a forgiveness F-bomb and let him go. I welcomed in the idea of releasing this relationship once and for all. I had been using the relationship as a crutch, and it was time for me to walk on my own.

My intuition guided me to take my time with this departure. Had I rushed through the breakup, I'd have been screwed. My ego would have nailed me with fear, self-attack, and second-guessing. Therefore I took my time to release him properly in my mind before I released the form of the relationship.

Once again I turned to the *Course* for help. The *Course* teaches that when we forgive, we're recognizing that whatever we think someone has done to us actually has not occurred. It's not about pardoning someone's wrongs; it's about seeing them as *not wrong* in the first place. I didn't fully comprehend this at first. Rather than let my logical mind figure it out, I brought it to my prayer and meditation. I prayed out loud, "~*ing,* help me forgive him and release him. Help me see him as innocent." Then I sat in a meditation in which I allowed my ~*ing* to create new thoughts and intervene with my ego. I visualized him entering into my meditation as I saw myself sending light from my heart to his heart. After a few minutes I began to see great rays of light pouring from the top of his head down to his toes. These same great rays of light were pouring from my head to my toes. I felt overwhelmed with a feeling of love. Eventually my image of our bodies was no longer visible, and all I could see was light. I felt at peace. All that was left was love.

Coming out of the meditation, I reflected on the experience through an ~*ing*-write. In my writing I came to realize that I didn't need to forgive my boyfriend for something he'd done. I was guided to do quite the opposite. My ~*ing* led me to see how false my attack and judgment had been. For instance, all my anger toward him was based on what I'd projected internally and perceived externally. My mind projected thoughts like "All men leave," "I'm not good enough," and "He's not giving me what I want." I was projecting my fear onto him, thereby perceiving him as a total asshole.

By realizing that I'd perceived this about him based on my own internal projector, I was able to begin to let him off the hook. This in turn led me to become even clearer about how my thoughts had created my reality. I came to realize that he was doing the best he could to manage his own ego's projections. I could now see how I'd forced my need to be saved onto a guy *who didn't want to save me*. Rather than realize this, I'd made him wrong for not meeting my ego's needs. This revelation offered me tremendous relief. As soon as I shifted my perception I began to see him with love. I saw him as innocent, accepted him, forgave him, and released him. I let great rays of light shine over the darkness.

The Holy Instant

My experience of releasing my boyfriend through the guidance of my ~ing is what the Course refers to as the "Holy Instant." The Holy Instant is the release of the illusion by way of forgiving the illusion itself. Once I recognized his innocence and saw my fear as the only problem, I was able to forgive the illusions my ego had created. The Holy Instant is the moment when we choose our ~ing instead of the ego as the teacher. By turning to my ~ing for guidance, I let love intervene through my mind. I called on spirit to help me see my boyfriend differently and to deepen my understanding of forgiveness.

This experience didn't just lead me to a deeper understanding of forgiveness—it showed me the true meaning of a miracle. The Course teaches that the shift in perception is a miracle. The moment I chose to perceive my boyfriend as innocent, I was able to love and accept him. In an instant, all my attack thoughts, judgment, separateness, hatred, and fear lifted. I experienced the Holy Instant. As the *Course* says, *"The holiest of all the spots on earth is where an ancient hatred has become a present love."* This present love was all I needed to release the illusion once and for all.

Letting Go

The Holy Instant prepared me to step up to the plate and face my biggest fear. After a morning spent in prayer and meditation, I headed to my boyfriend's apartment. With full confidence and love I told him how much I appreciated our time together and that I accepted that he wasn't able to give me what I wanted. I owned my part and apologized for controlling or manipulating the relationship in any way. My final words were, "I accept you, I forgive you, and I release you." He was somewhat disappointed but proud of me. He said, "That's the most mature breakup I've ever experienced." We hugged good-bye and agreed to remain good friends. I released him.

Slowing Down to Receive Guidance

This was the first time that I fearlessly walked away from a relationship without having another guy waiting in the wings. Most important, it was another step I'd taken toward truly understanding the meaning of forgiveness. I was proud of the work I'd done with Rha and my commitment to the *Course*.

In retrospect I can see how spirit was always guiding me. I was guided to the perfect assignment: the unavailable guy. Then my willingness to ask for help guided me to Rha, who would help me work through my limiting beliefs. Finally, I was guided through my meditation to choose my ~*ing* over my ego, forgive my boyfriend, and release him. The guidance was working through me the whole time. I was led to the Holy Instant.

We are always being guided, even though we often block it. The *Course* work opens us up to witness the guidance and co-create our lives with spirit. Each time we surrender and ask our ~*ing* for help, we will receive a loving response. Then we have to be present enough to receive it. The receiving step is crucial. The moment I stilled my mind through meditation, I was led to see my boyfriend as love and light. Had I chosen not to meditate, but instead to try to figure it all out on my own, I wouldn't have allowed the Holy Instant to occur. Receiving the Holy Instant happened in the midst of my stillness. Through prayer we surrender, and through meditation we receive guidance. I had to slow down in order to receive the miracle.

Practicing the Holy Instant

The *Course* teaches that you cannot bring the Holy Instant into your awareness if you don't want it: *"Your practice must therefore rest upon your willingness to let all littleness go."* Littleness is the plan of the ego. Our ego believes that there is a way to control the outcome of all situations through an outward action. Our *~ing* does the opposite by taking care of fearful thoughts internally. By turning inward for the miracle, we accept that spirit has a much better plan than we do, and we allow the guidance to flow.

All we need is to want the Holy Instant and fully release this desire to the care of our inner guide. The *Course* asks that we surrender *our* plans for happiness and let our *~ing* take over. By releasing our plan, we release the ego. The goal is to value no plan of the ego before the plan of our *~ing*. In the matter of ending my relationship, I prayed, meditated, and received. My willingness to release my ego's plan for happiness allowed my *~ing* to intervene. Choosing my *~ing* over my ego created the miracle of a loving breakup.

Daily Practice

The *Course* teaches: *"You can claim the holy instant anytime and anywhere you want it. In your practice, try to give over every plan you have accepted, for finding magnitude in littleness. It is not there. Use the holy instant only to recognize that you alone cannot know where it is, and can only deceive yourself."*

Each time we turn all conflict over to the care of our ~*ing* we experience an internal shift. We open the door for spirit to intervene and offer creative possibilities. These creative possibilities come through our mind in the form of thoughts like "Maybe I should see it his way," or "I have a part in this, too." These ~*ing*-driven thoughts allow us to see the situation with love and therefore bring in forgiveness as our primary tool for release. Through forgiveness we experience the Holy Instant, where *"an ancient hatred becomes a holy love."*

Accepting our ~*ing*'s plan on a daily basis will guide us to a feeling of inner peace. This is a simple practice. When you turn your thoughts over to your ~*ing*, you don't have to figure anything out. There is nothing complex about this. The only complexity is in your mind. Recognizing the simplicity of this practice supports our commitment to the Holy Instant.

The *Course* says: *"You could live forever in the Holy Instant, beginning now and reaching to eternity, but for a very simple reason. Do not obscure the simplicity of this reason, for, if you do, it will be only because you prefer not to recognize it, and not to let it go. The simple reason, stated simply as what it is: The Holy Instant is a time in which you receive and give perfect communication."*

By giving over our desires to the care of our inner guide, we will receive everything we need. The simplicity lies in the fact that our *~ing* is always right because spirit thoughts are based on love. With love there is an answer and a miraculous outcome for everything. Our job is to get into the practice of choosing love all the time. Since I'd been practicing thinking with my *~ing,* the step of choosing love began to be involuntary. This is the goal: to turn to love more often than to fear, so that one day, love is all that's left.

A Timeless Practice

This practice does not require time; it requires willingness. Once again, you don't have to *do* anything but be willing to receive guidance. Your willingness opens up your mind to communicate with the love of your *~ing.* When you're trying to make something happen, you're communicating with your ego. Your *~ing* won't ask you to change anything on the outside. Instead it will guide you to change your mind. Surrender your thoughts to your ~ing for help. By choosing to let spirit intervene, in a short time I was able to release an illusion that had been plaguing me for twenty-eight years. Choosing spirit is the path of least resistance—and the solution.

Our next step is to begin practicing the Holy Instant. By now you've become clear about your ego's patterns, surrendered them to your ~ing, asked for help, and turned your will over to the care of your inner guide. But as demonstrated by my story, the work doesn't end there. You need to stick around for the miracle! It's time to start practicing the Holy Instant in all our affairs. The more frequently we choose our ~ing, the more faith we'll have in the guidance we receive. The miraculous shift requires our faith because the shift is in our mind. Welcome in the Holy Instant and start to truly shift your perceptions and create miracles.

Communicating with Your ~ing

The *Course* teaches, "*Every thought you would keep hidden shuts communication off, because you would have it so.*" When you stop asking your ~ing for help you temporarily put the communication on hold. This was true for me for nearly three decades. I was stuck in my fearful relationship patterns because I wasn't allowing my ~*ing* to intervene. There was no potential for loving internal dialogue because I was letting my ego run this part of my life. But as soon as I seriously invited in my ~*ing* for help I was able to receive the guidance and open up the lines of communication.

In order to practice the Holy Instant, we need to communicate our desire for help. Begin communicating with your ~*ing* through prayer. Say out loud or in your mind, "Inner Guide, thank you for helping me see this with forgiveness, acceptance, and release."

The purpose of this prayer is to surrender your issue to the care of your ~*ing*. By truly giving it away, you receive guidance. The reason I suggest your prayer include the words "thank you" is that they imply that the prayer has already been taken care of. The words "thank you" reinforce our faith in spirit. Just be willing to ask for help and say the prayer out loud or in your mind. You can even write it on a piece of paper. Just put it out there and know that it's being heard.

Meditat~*ing*

Immediately after your prayer, sit in a meditation. I will guide you in this step through the written meditation below or through the meditation you can download from www .gabbyb.tv/meditate is titled "Great Rays Meditation." It is imperative that we calm our mind and allow our ~*ing* to come through. Otherwise our ego will think over the guidance. After asking your ~*ing* for help, continue the communication through meditation. The meditation step was powerful for me in creating the Holy Instant. In my meditation I was able to still my mind and clearly receive guidance.

Great Rays Meditation

To activate the Holy Instant, pray out loud or in your mind.

Then sit up straight in a seat or on the floor, with your palms facing upward.

Take a deep breath in through your nose and let it out through your mouth.

Continue this breathing throughout the meditation.

Hold in your mind the relationship that you need help with.

Identify the area in your body where you may be feeling discomfort around this situation.

Breathe deeply into that area of your body.

On the exhale, release.

Say in your mind, "I turn this fear over to my
   inner guide for transformation. I welcome the
   guidance."
Breathe in: I welcome guidance. I see you with
   light.
Breathe out: I release fear.
Breathe in: I choose love and light.
Breathe out: I accept this.
Breathe in: I welcome in great rays of healing
   light.
Breathe out: I choose to see only love and light.
Continue these mantras and allow your ~ing to
   guide your thoughts.

~ing-write

Right after your meditation, pick up your pen and begin
~ing-writing. Write at the top of the page, "How can I see
this with love?" Then begin freewriting.

Let your ~ing do her thing . . .

Where Is the Love?

Next, pay attention to where there is love in your ~*ing*-write. There may be some residual fear, but most likely the words coming through were compassionate and forgiving. Highlight the lines that resemble your willingness to forgive. Look closely at the love that you've offered up onto the page. This was the most enlightening step for me. When I chose to see love, I was able to see my boyfriend's innocence—he was doing the best he could. In addition, I was able to see how he'd become the victim of my illusion. By honestly witnessing your part in the situation, you'll come to see the innocence in others. Become clear about how your ego has created this illusion, and choose love over fear.

Let Your ~*ing* Host the Party in Your Mind

The *Course* says, "*In your practice, then, try only to be vigilant against deception, and seek not to protect the thoughts you would keep unto yourself. Let the Holy Spirit's purity shine them away, and bring all your awareness to the readiness for purity he offers you.*"

Now that you have the tools for creating the Holy Instant, it's up to you to invite it in. This thinking began to sink in for me because of my willingness to invite spirit in for help. The more I conversed with spirit through prayer and meditation, the more I allowed loving guidance to enter in. Allow your ~*ing* to host the party in your mind, and politely remind your ego that it's not on the guest list. Practicing the Holy Instant makes us host to love rather than hostage to fear.

Practicing the Holy Instant will prepare you to grow your relationship with spirit. In the coming chapter I'll share my experience of how I truly embraced spirit as my guide. As we continue on, stay connected to your prayer and meditation practice. Through this work you will receive more and more guidance to help you welcome a new way of perceiving the world. As you'll see in the coming chapter, choosing love over fear makes for awesome experiences.

Accepting
My Invitation

Seek to change nothing, but merely to accept

everything.

—A COURSE IN MIRACLES

•◦•

For more than fifteen years my mother has been living with a health condition. She spent a decade relying solely on holistic healing methods. Acupuncture, homeopathy, Reiki, juice cleansing, and a good old meditation practice did the trick for quite some time. Her willingness to receive alternative methods guided her to all kinds of unique health-care approaches. Most significantly, she was guided to a spiritual healer referred to as "John of God." This man is known throughout the world for performing miraculous healings, which can cure all types of life-threatening conditions and deepen one's spiritual connection.

Soon after she learned of this John of God, it turned out he was visiting the States and healing at The Omega Institute (a spiritual center) fifteen minutes from her home. She signed up immediately to visit him and receive a healing.

At first I balked at her plans to seek help from John of God. I chalked it up to one of my mom's hippie retreats. My ego judged her for not following the western approach to healing. Though I perceived myself as "open and spiritual," my ego clung to science and familiar healing methods as the primary treatments for diseases. Therefore I remained uncertain about her visit to see John of God from Brazil.

Despite my skepticism, she held fast to her belief. She visited John of God and came home beaming. Reflecting on the day, she spoke of the thousands of people dressed in white, powerful energy, and many miraculous healings. She'd watched John of God say a prayer over a woman in a wheelchair—within seconds the woman stood up and walked for the first time in years. His healing was shared through the exchange of energy and through powerful loving intention. People shared stories with my mother about how they recovered from cancer, depression, and many other life-threatening conditions. These stories empowered her and strengthened her faith in his work.

She went on to tell us about her personal experience with the healer. "He asked me to come to Brazil," she said. She explained that he invited certain people to visit him at his spiritual hospital in Brazil to receive further healing. My mother then exclaimed, "I know he can help me, and I'm going to Brazil."

"I'm going with you," I said. The words flooded out of my mouth. I had no idea why I was so quick to respond— it was as if someone were speaking through me. Everyone (including me) was confused by my instantaneous pledge. Only an hour earlier I was skeptical of John of God, and now I was signing myself up to travel across the world to see him?

Immediately I realized what I'd committed to, and felt a bit freaked out. I was not one to make impulsive decisions. But there was no turning back; my mother was already on the phone with the travel agent, booking our flights. She was thrilled to have a companion on her healing quest. I took her happiness as a sign that I was to accompany her and support her healing. Little did I know I was in for some major healing of my own.

Synchronicity

In the short time leading up to our trip, I received many signs of guidance. When I'd gotten in touch with Rha Goddess, she told me she'd be visiting John of God at the same time. In addition, several people mentioned his name in the months leading up to my trip, which was odd because I'd never heard of him prior to my mother's discovery. It didn't stop there: every part of the planning process was fully guided. The moment I decided to pick up the phone to coordinate some travel details, the travel guide contacted me out of the blue—at the exact moment I was calling her. Each time one of these synchronistic occurrences took place, I felt less and less skeptical. I saw them as signs of guidance.

Accepting My Invitation

We arrived in Brazil on March 15, 2008. The trip had awakened a lot of dormant feelings. I was reminded of my adolescent experience at the ashram; once again I was in a supercharged spiritual environment, surrounded by people seeking healing. At the ashram, however, I'd been largely unaware of my own energy and the energy of others. I'd also been in a much funkier place in my life, which led me to attract funky energy. I remembered what my mother told me about how I had the capacity to pick up other people's energy. Remembering this made all the difference: I was prepared. Not to mention I actually felt blessed with positive energy rather than weighed down by negative energy.

I was twenty-eight at the time of my visit to Brazil. At this point in my career, I was a full-time life coach and lecturer. I was teaching spirituality to the best of my ability, though in many ways I felt disconnected. I was teaching from my head rather than from my heart, which made me uncomfortable. I knew spirituality wasn't just about theology. It wasn't enough to understand the concepts on a detached, intellectual level. I wanted to *know* my own experience of spirit and teach from an authentic place.

The first night in Brazil, I spent hours journaling. At

one point I wrote, "I want to know what spirit really means to me." In that moment I signed another sacred contract with the Universe. I'd set a new intention through this written prayer, and man, oh man, was my prayer answered. By making this commitment I was accepting the invitation to know a deep spiritual connection.

Each day in Brazil brought new learning and miraculous occurrences. In the morning we'd visit the spiritual hospital where John of God performed his healings. I was drawn to this space like a magnet. Each time I approached the building I felt a rush of love come over me, as if energy was passing through my body. As the week went on, I felt more and more subtle yet astonishing physical sensations. My left hand started to feel numb, and my palm would heat up. This feeling of energy passing through my hand grew stronger each day. I brought this to the attention of the shaman who served as our guide. She replied, "That is beautiful, my dear. You're receiving the energy." She explained that I was feeling this energy in my left hand because it was my receiving hand. I didn't quite know what to make of this, but I accepted it and enjoyed the cool, unusual experience with an open mind.

I witnessed many auspicious occurrences. One morning I woke up inspired to paint. I painted a picture of my mother under a waterfall that flowed pink and red. This image represented the waterfall cleansing her. Her health condition was related to her blood; therefore I painted the water pink and red to represent a cleansing of the blood. Later that day we went on a guided hike. At the end of the path was a sacred spot they called the "holy waterfall." Each of us was to walk under the waterfall and ask for a blessing. I was behind my mother. I watched her stand exhilarated under the waterfall as the water washed over her—she was receiving a natural healing from the earth. I was overcome with joy when I realized the image I'd painted was right in front of me in physical form.

This waterfall was just one of many miraculous sights. I saw double rainbows, I saw water boil without being heated, and I witnessed incredible healing moments. But none of what I saw with my eyes compared with what I saw in my meditation. While in Brazil we spent many hours in deep meditation. We'd sit in large groups and meditate while John of God performed his healing. He would heal and bless hundreds of people a day. He explained to us that the group's collective meditation supported his work. Our intention and energy helped sustain him as he healed others.

Though we were serving John of God through our meditation, we were also receiving our own healing. I was taught that many past wounds are healed through meditation. For instance, I experienced a mind-blowing meditation in which I was walking on the beach in Martha's Vineyard with my father. We were holding hands, smiling and laughing. This image represented release and forgiveness. In that short meditation I was gifted with the Holy

Instant of seeing my father as only love, and releasing all my past resentments. I came out of the meditation and said to my mother, "I've forgiven Dad. I've released my past resentments. It's over." From that day forward my relationship with my father has been beautifully transformed. In one meditation I was able to release twenty-eight years of ego projections. I was guided to forgive.

My Request

When you visit John of God for healing, you're asked to bring a clear intention of what you'd like healed. You can request anything from a physical healing to the release of an old thought system. My request was clear: *I want to deepen my spiritual connection. I want to know spirit.* I wrote this message on a piece of paper, held the intention in my mind, and went before him to offer up my request. He smiled as my request was translated from English to Portuguese. He responded, "You're being guided to know spirit." I immediately began to receive clear signs of guidance. The response to my request came in many forms.

I spent the last week in Brazil filled with love and with my newfound connection to spirit. The feeling of energy entering into my left hand became constant. I began to feel as though someone were holding my hand almost all the time. As totally wacky as this seemed on the surface, I was surprised by how comfortable I felt. The feeling of this presence grew stronger when I sat in meditation. Whenever I sat, I felt an unmistakable rush of love through my whole body. My anxiety would lift immediately, and my body felt as if it were wrapped in a warm blanket. While in Brazil I found myself sitting in three- to four-hour meditations. Time flew by.

I also began to feel this presence of spirit come to me through my thoughts. While in Brazil I'd hear my inner voice speak loudly and more clearly than ever. The thoughts I heard no longer sounded like mine; for instance, I kept hearing an inner voice say, *Stay connected to the light. Keep inviting in the light and love of spirit.*

This voice connected to me through my writing, as well. On the last night of our trip I stayed up late writing. As I wrote I began to notice that the words coming through me were no longer mine. Then my hand started to move involuntarily. The writing became rapid and the diction seemed foreign. At first this freaked me out, but I went with it. As my hand scribbled quickly across the page, clear guidance came through. I wrote: "Stay connected to spirit at all times. Everything you're seeking is in the light of spirit. Your work is to be one with spirit so you can heal others." The writing became illegible as it spilled onto the page. I underlined this passage and made another commitment to keep this spirit connection alive.

The people in Brazil suggested that in order to feel this

connection to spirit when I returned home, all I needed to do was to invite spirit in. This message reinforced the *Course's* Holy Instant. I understood the Holy Instant on a deeper level now. It became clear that the more I called on spirit, the greater my awareness to the loving guidance around me became. This spiritual connection was the beginning of a serious relationship with my inner guide.

My deep desire to know spirit led me to truly believe in a power greater than myself. This power was no longer a concept from a book, a suggestion from a friend, or a cute gerund I referred to as *~ing*. It became a presence that I could no longer deny.

Hanging Out in the Light

Upon arriving back in New York, I feared that I'd lose this connection. So I took the Brazilians' advice and invited spirit into every area of my life. Spirit, aka *~ing*, became my closest companion. Whenever I felt uncertain, fearful, physically ill, or stuck in ego, I'd turn to spirit for help. I talked to spirit upon waking and before going to sleep. I'd connect to spirit before a date, a business meeting, a hard workout, or a night out with friends. I found that by inviting spirit into my life I enhanced all my experiences. Relying on my inner guide became instinctive and natural. The more I called on spirit, the more love I felt around me. My continued willingness to welcome this presence deepened my spiritual connection daily.

As my spiritual connection strengthened, my meditations became super trippy. I started to feel guidance more physically, hear my ~*ing* more clearly, and see the world in an entirely different way. I'd see sparks of light with my eyes closed. These sparks resembled the supportive presence I knew was always with me. Then I began noticing these same sparks when my eyes were open. They were like laser beams of light. I'd reactivated the spiritual connection I felt through my high school meditations. The important difference was that this time I wasn't afraid of it. I could now work with this powerful energy to enrich my life.

Knowing Spirit Has My Back

It became clear to me that this inner guidance system was like a GPS for life. Each time I'd come up against some kind of issue, I'd turn inward for help. My ~*ing* guided my romantic relationships, business deals, and daily interactions. I was also guided to take care of my health in a new way. My addictive patterns began to subside. The years I spent tormented by issues around food—overeating and obsessing about calories—were over. Within a few short years those issues seemed to disappear. I no longer needed food or a relationship or a credential to fill me up. I was finally full.

This feeling of guidance also supported my self-confidence. Now that I understood that all the love and safety I needed was inside me, I could stop searching for it. I no longer felt the desperate need to be accepted, to seem cool, and to prove myself to the world. That's not to say that I was totally released from those patterns, but they did change dramatically. I no longer needed anything on the outside to complete me. This inner connection was all I needed. My daily practice of connecting to spirit helped me maintain positive energy. Because my energy vibrated at a positive frequency, I was attracting more positivity. Knowing how to access this state was all I needed. I felt clear-minded, calm, and powerful. Whenever I lost track of this feeling, I'd bring myself back to equilibrium through meditation and prayer. Having this connection was all I needed.

Physical Healing

Deepening my spiritual connection greatly enhanced my physical body, too. I felt more energized, stronger. In addition, for years I'd lived with a hernia. By this point in my spiritual growth I wanted to patch up this area of my body. Metaphorically, it felt leaky. John of God reinforced the message that spirit was always working through our western doctors and never to shy away from traditional medicine.

Therefore I scheduled a surgery for December of 2009 (one month before the launch of *Add More ~ing to Your Life*). A week before the scheduled surgery, I woke up to a loud inner voice saying, *Postpone the surgery until after the book tour.* Spirit's communication was clear and to the point. I had full faith in this message, and I called my mother to tell her about my *~ing*Tervention. My mother replied, "I've been expecting this call." She went on to tell me that one day earlier she, too, had heard an inner voice. Her *~ing* said, "Gabrielle won't be having her surgery at this time." This brilliant synchronicity sealed the deal. I called my doctor immediately and postponed the surgery. In retrospect I can see clearly why spirit intervened. Had I undergone the surgery at that time, I'd have been totally screwed because my book shipped early and I was called in to do several speaking engagements and TV appearances. Remember, spirit has a much better plan for us than we do. Now that I had a clear connection with spirit, I could allow these *~ing*Terventions to occur and receive valuable guidance in all areas of my life.

Being a Messenger

It soon became clear that I couldn't hoard this connection for myself. I had to honor the message I received in my writing and *work with spirit to help heal others.* I did just that.

As I became more confident in my connection to spirit, I invited my coaching clients to sit with me in meditation and share in this experience. Some clients loved this so much that we'd meditate for hours over our scheduled time together. Each woman I coached had been guided to me much as I'd been guided to my coach, Rha. It was clear that we all had work to do together. My clients approached my spiritual guidance with open minds and hearts. Rather than freak out in reaction to my "out there" suggestions, they paid attention and got excited. Their faithful response to my teaching was a beautiful mirror for my own faith in my spiritual connection. And as the *Course* says, *"To teach is to learn."* Therefore, each woman I taught strengthened my own faith and practice.

Seeing Sparks

The sparks I saw in my meditation began to show up in my outward vision all the time. Whenever I was around certain people or in certain spiritual communities, I'd see these sparks of light. At times I felt as though I were witnessing the world from afar, standing across the street and watching myself experience life. The world looked brighter and life began to flow. These sacred experiences reinforced my faith in spirit on a daily basis.

Building Your Own Relationship with Spirit

The *Course* teaches, *"Let your self be one with something beyond it."* I posted this quote on my desk as a daily reminder to turn inward and embrace my spiritual connection. This was my experience. You will have your own. As much as I want to be a spiritual cheerleader, I will refrain from pushing you in any specific direction. We all have a spiritual connection of our own understanding. My connection to spirit may be similar to yours—or completely different. Know that there is no right or wrong way to connect. Some people may feel spirit when they get the chills. Others may feel an intuitive knowing that reminds them of a greater connection. There are all kinds of ways to experience spirit, and there is no right or wrong connection.

Keep in mind that your ego will resist these moments of connection. When I began feeling the energy pass through my left hand, my ego tried to convince me that there was something physically wrong with me. I intuitively knew that this was not a physical condition, but rather a spiritual connection, and I chose to listen to let my ~*ing* intervene. The brighter my light began to shine, the harder my ego had to work to keep the darkness alive. Therefore I continued to rev up my connection to spirit and release my ego one thought at a time.

One thing to remember when opening up to spirit is that we can often experience some pain in our chakras. A chakra is an energy center, and we have seven of them, each one in a different area of our body. When these chakras are open, it means there is positive energy flow; when they are closed, it means we are emotionally stuck in some way. In our bodies we carry old pain from the past and hold it deep within our muscles and in every cell. Holding this negativity leads to disease and illness. When we invite spirit into our life, these pockets of negativity begin to break open. Sometimes we can literally feel the chakras open up as the stuck energy passes through us. Be conscious of these experiences and embrace them, knowing that this feeling is part of the process.

Remember that as you open your mind to a spiritual connection, your body will reap the benefits. In my case I began to have more energy, released pain in my joints, and saw several health conditions disappear. I no longer need certain prescription drugs that I once relied on. As my mind healed, my body followed. When we release fear and negativity from our minds, they are no longer projected onto our bodies. In my case, I became more conscious of my physical body and how my mind was affecting it. The *Course* says, *"Do not ask Spirit to heal the body. Ask rather that Spirit teach you the right perception of the body."*

This concept was key to my mother's healing. After

visiting John of God her physical condition actually got worse. Often things get worse before they get better, so that the underlying issues can come to the surface and be acknowledged. The severity of her condition helped her to connect more deeply to her spirit. As a result, my mother was led to the right doctor who would be her guide throughout her healing process. (Remember that spirit works through people.) But this was only part of the guidance. The primary guidance she received was through her mind. As she embarked on a year's worth of serious medication, she continuously called on spirit for guidance. This call was answered through many miraculous internal shifts. For instance, my mother had spent the majority of her life caring for others, and for the first time she allowed herself to be cared for. This experience was part of spirit's intervention, as it was a necessary step in the healing of her mind. Her year spent undergoing the medication was one of the most peaceful times in her life. Many of her past emotional hangups shifted and she regained faith in spirit. Since then, regardless of the status of her condition, she lives fearlessly. Her right perception of her physical condition is her healing. Today she coexists with it peacefully. Though she still lives with this condition, she knows why. She understands the ways in which this condition has been an assignment in her life, and honors this experience as her qualifier to knowing the true meaning of a spiritual connection. What's cooler than that?

Accept Your Invitation

Now it's time to open up to your own experience of spirit. By this point in your journey you may or may not have felt your ~ing's guidance. Maybe your ego's been too strong for you to notice, or maybe it felt unnatural to think in this way. Though you may have resisted your ~ing, you still may have noticed unique synchronicities or guidance of some kind. Pay attention to the ways you've experienced this Universal guidance in your own life. For example, maybe there is a story behind how you found this book. After publishing my first book I received several e-mails from people saying things like "The book literally fell off the shelf," or "My mother bought the book for me right when I needed it." My response to these e-mails was, "You read it when you need it." As soon as you're willing to receive guidance, the help will come in a form that resonates with you. These types of scenarios reinforce our recognition of the presence of guidance around us. Remember that we're always being guided.

Regardless of your spiritual or religious background, you're entitled to welcome more guidance into your life. The suggested exercises throughout the book thus far have warmed you up to accept your own invitation from spirit. Your inner guide has been beckoning you for years, and now it's time to listen. In the coming steps I'll guide you to pay attention to your ~ing and witness the guidance. I'll offer you tools for unblocking any resistance to this presence, and I'll guide you to listen to the messages you receive. Whatever issue you may be struggling with, whatever problem you may be suffering from, there is a spiritual solution. When you welcome spirit into your life and accept your invitation, you'll know a new way of being and a life beyond your wildest dreams. Fear will lift; anxiety, resentment, and attachment will slip away. You'll feel a presence greater than yourself leading you on a path toward true serenity and peace. You'll know that all your obstacles are opportunities, and you'll learn to lean on a power greater than yourself. Most important, you'll no longer feel the need to figure life out. You'll just *be*.

STEP 1. SAY YES TO SPIRIT

The *Course* teaches, *"Love will immediately enter into any mind that truly wants it."* This was the case for me. All it took for me to deepen my connection to my spirit was the desire to know more. My request to John of God was a statement to the Universe that I was ready to accept an authentic connection to spirit. My call for spirit allowed me to receive. Each of us has an infinite capacity to receive spiritual guidance; we just need to be open to letting it in.

If you feel ready to accept your own spiritual invitation, it's time to sign a sacred contract. All that is required is a commitment to receive. Don't be afraid of this invitation. You will have your own unique experience with spirit. We all have an inner guide connecting in a way that we are capable of receiving. My connection happened to come through meditation and writing, and primarily by physically receiving energy. For others it may be as simple as a strong intuition or receiving guidance through other people. This step isn't going to dictate how you receive, but it will blast open consciousness of the guidance that is around you. You will receive in whatever way your inner guide feels is appropriate for you.

If you're ready to accept your spiritual invitation, let's create a sacred contract with the Universe. Write a letter to your inner guide. In your own words, invite your *~ing* to become more present in your life. Clearly acknowledge that you're ready to know more and you're willing to receive guidance. Then sign the contract and close it with a thank-you. Thank your *~ing* for the guidance and support.

STEP 2. UNBLOCK

The more you believe in this contract, the more you will receive. Keep in mind that your ego will want to judge this experience. Ego will lead you to believe that the guidance you're receiving is all coincidental happenstance. In other cases your ego will convince you that your desire to connect with your spirit is unwarranted and impossible. It is important to pay attention to your ego at this time. Do your best to forgive yourself for getting hooked into the ego's fear, and continue to release all blocks.

The most powerful way to unblock yourself from receiving guidance is through daily prayer and meditation. Remember: prayer is the time to ask, and meditation is the time to listen. The reason I have kept my connection to spirit alive is that I invite spirit into my life every day and listen for the guidance. Remove your ego's blocks daily with a dedicated prayer and meditation practice. This practice is simple. Begin each day by turning your will and your life over to the care of your ~ing. This is a great time to use the prayer I referenced from the *Course* in chapter 4: *"Where would you have me go? What you would have me do? What would you have me say? And to whom?"* Then simply sit in a five-minute meditation and listen to the voice of your inner guide. Begin your meditation by breathing in *I welcome guidance*, and breathing out *I will receive*.

STEP 3. LISTEN

Once again it's time to meditate. You've signed your sacred contract and now you will receive more guidance. I was able to hear the guidance because I made a daily commitment to still my mind through meditation. If you've been strug-gling with the meditations, give yourself a break and keep it simple. This chapter's meditation assignment is easy. You don't need to turn on an audio recording or follow a writ-ten guide. All you need do is nothing. Just sit in stillness. Your desire to listen to the guidance is all you need. Offer yourself a minimum of five minutes in the morning and five minutes at night to sit in complete stillness. Listen to what comes through. Listen without judgment.

Getting into the practice of welcoming, unblocking, and listening to spirit will help you strengthen your relationship with your ~ing. There is no need to define this relationship: just allow it to occur. Stay open for signs of guidance and enjoy the love.

The more you welcome spirit into your life, the more fulfilled you will feel. Becoming spiritually full is the focus of the upcoming chapter. Know that each lesson is guiding you farther along the path of filling your ego's emptiness with the everlasting love of spirit.

PART 3

The Miracle

9

Spirit Became My Boyfriend

To heal is to make happy.

—A COURSE IN MIRACLES

◆—◆

My meditation pillow became my favorite place to hang. I spent hours sitting with ambient music playing in the background, or sometimes in complete silence. In addition to my awesome meditation practice, I amped up my *Course* study, thereby strengthening my relationship with my *~ing*. Each time I called on the spirit of my *~ing*, I'd release the ego. The *Course* says, *"This Call is so strong that the ego always dissolves at its sound. This is why you must choose to hear one of two voices within you."* The *Course* teaches that the mind cannot serve two masters. Realizing I could no longer function with a split mind, I was able to commit fully to spirit's guidance. Therefore I continuously chose my *~ing*, and I became more and more happy.

Right Mind

I came to understand that restoring my thoughts back to love wasn't a one-time gig. It had to become a moment-to-moment practice of turning my fears over to my ~ing. The *Course* says, *"Our task is but to continue, as fast as possible, the necessary process of looking straight at all the interference and seeing it exactly as it is."* Therefore, each time fear crept in, my ~ing would intervene to help me see it wasn't real. Practicing the *Course* work daily made this way of perceiving the world almost involuntary. This way of thinking is what the *Course* refers to as "right-mindedness," which occurs when we perceive fear as an opportunity to forgive and restore our thoughts back to love. Each time I witnessed an attack thought, a judgment, or a sense of lacking, I saw it as a call for love and asked my ~ing for help. My inner guide led me to forgive these thoughts and recognize them as illusions, thereby relinquishing the separation and reconnecting my mind with love.

Thinking this way showed me how much power I had over my own personal experience and how my thoughts greatly affected the rest of the world. For instance, when I felt disconnected from someone, I would send him or her loving intentions and immediately feel connected again. Or when I felt powerless over a situation, I'd turn to my ~ing for help and feel empowered the moment my thoughts returned to love. Each time I turned inward for help, I received guidance and strengthened my right-mindedness. The "right mind" or miracle-mindedness is when our mind is faithful to love. When we think this way we believe in love, so we instinctively choose it when faced with conflict. This way of thinking is based on a be-lief system far beyond the ego—it's based on love.

My New Relationship

Each day spent in prayer and meditation deepened my relationship with my spirit. This relationship was fulfill-ing, nurturing, inspiring, loving, honest, and faithful. This was the relationship I'd been searching for all my life. I soon realized that all the love and support I'd been lusting after in a man was inside me all along. The clas-sic line "all the love you need is inside you" was true! For years I secretly wanted to believe in that philosophy, but I couldn't fully comprehend it until I lived it. My dedica-tion to spirit led me inward to a true source of love and safety. I was no longer looking for love—*I was living in love.*

Comfort

I felt an overarching sense of comfort when I connected to my ~*ing.* As soon as I centered into my meditation I'd feel as though I were wrapped in a warm blanket. I felt the pres-ence of spirit through my thoughts, experiences, and even physical senses.

Whenever I felt fearful or anxious, I'd turn to my meditation pillow or say a prayer and connect to the spirit of my inner guide. Within seconds, spirit would blast through the fear and help me reconnect with the feeling of love. I felt this presence rush through my limbs and fill me with serenity and peace. It was like I had a built-in Xanax without ever popping a pill. What's most lifting and satisfying is that this sense of peace is always available. I now had a relationship with spirit that filled me with love. There was an infinite amount of love to call on at any given moment: all I had to do was ask. This connection provided me with security and a sense that I was always being taken care of.

Security

I had lived most of my life in fear. Now, for the first time ever, I was at peace. It actually felt odd. My ego resisted this sense of security by trying to convince me that it was too good to be true and that the awesomeness would disappear as soon as I faced a major challenge. But my connection to spirit was too strong for the ego. Whenever my ~ing sensed ego doubt, spirit would intervene and save me from my old fearful way of being. The presence of spirit was protecting me from fear.

I finally felt safe. The security I was seeking in a romantic partner was now available to me through my connection to spirit. All my codependent analysis showed me that I was desperately seeking someone to save me. At last my need to be saved dissolved and I finally felt secure. This sense of security came from within, and I knew it would never leave me. I no longer had to search for safety on the outside because I was totally taken care of from within.

Loving Experiences

The presence of spirit came through not only on my meditation pillow, but in every area of my life. I experienced many moments of love that I had been unable to access before. Many of these experiences came through some kind of physical activity or while spending time in nature. In the middle of a long run I'd feel love rush through me. I'd feel it while hiking in the woods, swimming in the ocean, or walking in the park. In the midst of these physical activities I'd be taken over by a sense of joy and peace. Outdoor physical activity became a beautiful catalyst for igniting my inner spirit. Moving in nature really turned my ~ing on.

As I listened to my intuition, I was guided to many other loving experiences. One afternoon I was overwhelmed with work. In the midst of a potential breakdown I heard my ~ing say, *Stop working and go to the coffee shop.* I followed this inspired thought and walked over to the café on my corner. I ordered a soy-milk latte, as usual. As soon as I paid my bill I turned around to find one of my childhood friends sitting in the corner. She was visiting from out of town and staying for less than forty-eight hours. We were thrilled to reunite, and we spent the next three hours sitting together in the coffee shop, catching up. Within minutes of seeing her, my work anxiety disappeared and I restored my right-mindedness. When I returned to work, my ~*ing* was back on and my inner peace was restored. Spirit had led me to this loving experience and taken me out of my own way.

Witnessing these loving experiences showed me how divinely guided I'd become. These kinds of moments always had been available in the past, but I'd been too blocked to notice them. My old way of living would have let my ego trample over my intuition and I'd have shrugged off the guidance to go to the coffee shop. Or, more likely, I wouldn't have heard the message in the first place. My relationship with spirit had become so strong I was able to receive the guidance and experience many loving, miraculous occurrences.

Inspiration

The relationship I created with my ~*ing* was full of inspiration. Each time I sat in meditation or called on my ~*ing* through prayer, I received an inspired response. It's often said that when you're inspired, you're "inspirit."

Through my spiritual practice I'd cleared space to receive inspiration daily. My connection with spirit rocketed inspiration through me.

This inspiration came in handy while writing my first book, *Add More ~ing to Your Life*. At the onset of the writing process I invited spirit to intervene. I asked for inspiration throughout the writing process. I'd never written a book, and therefore a lot of ego crap crowded my mind. Rather than freak out, I turned the fear over to my *~ing* and let the guidance move through me. I began a daily prayer practice of releasing my writing fears over to the care of my inner guide. As a result of turning my fears over, I was fully taken care of. Each time I sat down to write, I asked my *~ing* to enter in. This invitation ignited my connection with spirit, at which point inspiration began to flow. Some nights I'd stay up very late writing. My fingers moved fast across the keyboard as my thoughts poured onto the page. I could feel an inner voice working through me. Thanks to my constant contact with my spirit, the writing process was fluid and actually fun. Calling on my spirit eliminated all doubt and never failed to provide me with the inspiration I was seeking.

Once again my *~ing* had filled me with something I'd been chasing on the outside. I no longer needed to rely on a romantic partner to feel inspired. All I had to do was stay connected to my *~ing* and let the inspiration flow.

Support and Guidance

With spirit I could do anything. I felt supported uncondi-
tionally by my inner voice of love. Whenever I got caught
in an ego tornado, spirit always had my back. If I ever
veered off track, something would happen to knock some
sense into me or I'd be hit over the head with clear direction back to love. Whenever my work or personal situations
were held up for any reason, my ego would get frustrated
and nasty. But when I reflected on the outcomes, I'd immediately see how spirit intervened in the holdup.

This type of guidance came when I was trying to get
a signature on an important contract. For some reason
the lawyers were delayed and the deal points were difficult
to negotiate. It was taking many more weeks than I'd expected. My ego was freaking out, trying to convince me
that I'd lose the deal or that something would go wrong.
When we finally agreed to terms and were about to sign
the agreement, another opportunity came in. It was divine
timing because I needed to include a clause in the original
agreement that would allow me to participate in both projects. Had I signed a day earlier, I would have been locked
out of the other deal. It became clear to me that spirit was
playing a role in this holdup. Guidance comes in many

forms, even when things seem not to be moving the way we want. The *Course* reminds us that spirit has a much better plan for us than we do. This type of guidance began to happen all the time—so often that I came to accept and embrace any holdups or setbacks.

Loneliness Disappeared

I now felt as though I had an internal companion with me at all times. Turning to my *~ing* regularly meant I never felt alone. I'd longed for this feeling since adolescence. Now that I was united with love on the inside, I always felt connected to something and my loneliness lifted. I truly enjoyed just being with spirit. I'd crave that time spent alone in my apartment in meditation, listening to music, writing, or drawing. I'd leave parties early to go home and meditate. I valued this time spent in silence with spirit.

Spirit Showed Up for Me

All my life I'd ached desperately to be heard. My new relationship with spirit solved that problem. Each time I asked my *~ing* for guidance, I received an inspired response. Once again these responses came in the forms of an inner voice, stream-of-consciousness writing, inspired intuition, and brilliant synchronicities. It felt good to be heard at last. As long as I was patient I'd receive the response. I learned that when I'd get impatient and try to control the response in any way, I'd block it. Instead I asked for help and patiently waited for my ~*ing* to respond. Rather than push and scream to be heard by the world, I now simply turned inward, and I always received a response.

I Found "It"

I had fallen in love with spirit. This was a love I'd never known before. I'd become full with inner peace. Since I was no longer searching for love and fulfillment in a romantic partner, I was able to let men off the hook. And because I no longer expected my parents or friends to save me, I could let them off the hook, too. I could now enjoy my relationships for exactly what they were at any given time. I was able to release my major expectations and allow people to be the best they could. I was full of spirit and complete. For the first time in my life I understood the meaning of true love. I now knew that love was not a onetime feeling I could access from a boyfriend. Love is in everything. I felt the presence of love in nature, in the company of a new friend, reading a book, or riding a bike. Love was not something to be acquired; it was something I always had. I learned that love is unselfish and abundant. The love supply is infinite; it can't ever run out. You can either be aware of it or not. All I had to do was sit in meditation, smile at a stranger, perform a random act of kindness, or think with my ~ing, and I'd reactivate my awareness of love. My relationship with spirit guided me to *"release the blocks to the awareness of love's presence."*

The Bridge

In this stage of my spiritual development I was in a place referred to by the *Course* as the "bridge." The bridge is *"the distance between illusion and truth, perception and knowledge."* This bridge is described as spirit's vision of peace and forgiveness. It is a transition in our perspective on reality—this transition is from the fear of the ego back to heaven: the inner state of knowing love. At this time I felt as though I really was walking over a bridge from my old life into a new world—and I wasn't walking alone. I was literally surrounded by the presence of spirit escorting me over the bridge. The *Course* says, *"Truth has rushed to meet you since you called upon it. If you knew who walks beside you on the way that you have chosen, fear would be impossible."* I now knew I had a companion, a guide, a teacher, and a friend. Through the guidance of spirit I exchanged my dark fears for miracles and continued to walk over the bridge.

Healing

My faith in spirit was the answer to all my life's problems. From codependent addictions to physical conditions, I was healing. The *Course* has a magnificent line that inspired me throughout this healing process: *"Can you imagine what it means to have no cares, no worries, no anxieties, but merely to be perfectly calm and quiet all the time?"* A year ago this would have sounded like a pipe dream. Now it was my reality. My worries and anxieties had evaporated. I was calm.

Spreading the Love

My mind was being restored to what the *Course* calls "true perception." The *Course* describes this as the experience of true communication in our right minds, allowing spirit to be shared through us. It became clear that I had to use this spirit connection to strengthen my commitment to serve others. I had cleared space within my own mind to receive love, and now it was time to share it.

My connection to the love of spirit was reflected back to me in many ways. One in particular was the response to my work. My coaching groups grew larger, and my lecture halls were packed. While teaching and lecturing, I found it incredibly easy to speak extemporaneously. I'd write an outline for a lecture and bag it at the door. I could riff for hours on the topic of love and spirit. I could answer every question that came at me. This was easy. The answers were always the same. It all came down to love.

The women in my community were continually reaching out for help. There came a point at which I was no longer able to mentor and guide each of them individually. I had a hard time saying no to their calls for help. So I turned inward for advice. I asked my ~ing how I could share this love with the masses and not totally burn out. My ~ing replied, *Get online!* This was the solution! Right away spirit guided me to create a social networking website called Her-Future.com for women to find mentors and be mentors.

Through the Internet I was able to hold space for a community of women connecting, serving, and loving one another. The site was a hit from the get-go. Thousands of women became members and began to carry the conversation. Each time I'd log on to the site I'd feel a rush of love come over me. Women created groups (Power Posses) based on topics ranging from health and wellness to shared prayer. Love was bleeding through the computer screen. This website reinforced my newfound knowledge of the fact that love is in everything. I learned that the energy and intention behind this site traveled through the Internet. Whoever needed to find the site would find it and use it as a guide back to love. I received thousands of e-mails from women saying things like "I found this site right when I needed it." Little did they know, spirit got them there. Spirit was working through the site to guide us to heal one another.

The powerful connections I now had with the women in my life filled me up even more. I felt a fiery spark within my community. These relationships illustrated a lesson from the *Course* based on the special love relationship. The *Course* teaches us to make our brotherly relationships (friendships) more romantic and our romantic relationships more brotherly. That was what was going on for me. Because I now found romance and sparks within my companionable relationships, I was able to take even more pressure off men. This was another way spirit worked through me to overcome my codependent patterns. I now understood the true meaning of having romantic brotherly relationships.

Had I told anyone that I was in a relationship with spirit, they'd have freaked. When I tried to explain this connection to my friends, they resisted it. That didn't matter. I honored their processes and recognized that their egos couldn't comprehend what was going on for me. I understood this because I, too, never would have been able to grasp this awesomeness without firsthand experience. Odd as these experiences sounded to others, they felt more right to me than anything I'd ever known. My spiritual connection helped me trust myself, enabling me to release all those who resisted my newfound ways of being. I trusted my inner guidance and didn't allow skepticism to influence my flow. I welcomed the feeling of peace and unconditional love.

Your Relationship with Spirit

It is important to acknowledge once again that everyone has a spirit connection of his or her own understanding. Even those people who have full faith in the ego connect to spirit without even realizing it—possibly through their love of a musical instrument or playing sports with friends. Think about those moments when you feel chills pass through your body or you experience wild synchronicity. This chapter's work will be dedicated to becoming conscious of our own personal relationship with spirit. Throughout the book we've been strengthening our relationship with spirit, and now it's time to witness how that relationship has grown. I'll encourage you to look closely at the ways spirit has intervened in your life—how you've been guided and when you're most connected. By paying attention to these moments you'll become more mindful of participating rather than rushing past. I can think back to many moments in my life when spirit was trying to intervene, but I just wouldn't slow down enough to listen. The goal of this chapter is learning to pay attention. Become the witness of spirit in your own life in order to become more conscious of this connection and do your part to enhance the relationship. Growing this relationship will provide you with the entire fulfillment you desire so you can live with ease.

Watering the Plant

The exercises thus far have been like seeds planted for you to grow your relationship with spirit. Now it's time to water the plant you have created. Each time you honor spirit, your relationship grows stronger. Think about it with regard to interpersonal relationships. If you're ignoring all the love you receive from someone, you may lose track of the connection. Spirit is available to all of us, all the time, and it's our job to pay attention to the connection and allow it to grow.

STEP 1. PAY ATTENTION

To become more conscious of how spirit connects to you, let's begin with a list. Make a list of all the ways you experience spirit. If you are unsure, use these examples as guidelines. Possibly you feel spirit as chills running through your body, a strong intuition, synchronicity, or an inner voice. You may experience spirit as a rush of love coming over you when you're with certain people or in certain situations.

Often people feel spirit through physical activity, such as after a long run or while dancing. Pay attention to the times when you feel a connection to a power greater than yourself. Make this list and become consciously aware of when spirit pats you on the back.

STEP 2. BE MINDFUL

Now that you have your list, it is important to be mindful of these moments. Instead of rushing past them, take them in. Allow yourself to swim in the feeling of love. There was nothing cooler than my time spent soaking up the love of spirit through meditation or exercise. Become still, and welcome the presence into your mind and body. Allow spirit to pass through you, and enjoy the connection.

STEP 3. ADD WATER

Now it's time to add water by activating spiritual encounters. For instance, if you know that you can access a spirit connection through ~ing-writing, then ~ing-write. If you know you can access spirit through yoga, unroll your mat. Take time out of your day to choose to spend time with spirit. This commitment to connect to spirit is like taking care of a plant—you must add water for it to grow.

♦   ♦   ♦

As you strengthen your relationship to spirit, you will begin to feel more complete from the inside out. This is when you start to release attachments and extend a confident energy of inner peace. In my case, exuding this wholeness magnetized people and situations that were equally healthy. As my relationship to spirit grew greater and greater, my relationships with other people followed suit. In the coming chapter you will see how in our completeness we call in healthy relationships that reflect our inner light. This is what the *Course* calls the "holy relationship."

10

Love Wins

The holiness of your relationship forgives you
both, undoing the effects of what you both
believed and saw.

—A COURSE IN MIRACLES

◆

he comfort, security, inspiration, support, and love I received from spirit was everything I'd been searching for in a man. Now that I had access to this spirit connection, I was truly fulfilled. I shone from the inside out. My friends and family regularly remarked on how chilled out and relaxed I'd become—they referred to me as "calm" and "centered," which was totally new. This was amazing because for most of my life I'd been a complete head case. Now that I'd connected to spirit, the people who surrounded me reflected back my calm internal state. Oddly, this transition felt natural. I was able to gracefully shed my old frantic way of being and embrace my new chilled-out approach to life. I welcomed this new perception.

As a result of my inner shift, the Universe began sending me many gifts. My career was moving forward fast. My friendships deepened, and new romantic opportunities fell in my lap. I was vibrating at such a high frequency that my energy was magnetizing greatness. I was now attracting amazing, available men who really wanted to be with me. The fact that I was calling in this type of man showed me how much I had transformed. I was no longer putting out a needy vibe or desperately seeking safety in someone else. I was now complete, inspired, and whole. Therefore, I was meeting awesome men who dug me as much as I dug myself. My inner light was shining outward and everyone felt it.

Spirit Had a Better Plan

Though I was super happy being single, spirit guided me back into a relationship. It gradually became clear that I had things to learn by being in a relationship. There are times in our lives when the finest learning and healing occur while we're on our own, whereas at other times spirit directs us to the perfect romantic partner for the best growth opportunity. In this case I was guided to revisit an old relationship—the guy who I'd peacefully broken up with a year earlier. I never could have expected this; I thought it was over for good. I knew from my *Course* study that the relationship had never ended on a spiritual level, but that the form of the relationship had just changed. Even though we'd been physically apart for more than a year, we'd been spiritually connected: the energetic connection between us never died.

I often felt his energy while sitting in meditation. My *~ing* would guide me to loving thoughts about him, which would bring up loving feelings, and hours later he'd e-mail me, saying, "Thinking about you." The entire time we spent physically apart, we remained energetically connected. As soon as we both released the relationship fully, spirit could intervene and lead us to what was truly right. And as the Universe would have it, we were brought back together. I welcomed the assignment, knowing that spirit would do for me what I couldn't do for myself. I knew for sure I couldn't have planned this!

I was guided back to him to experience what the *Course* calls the "holy relationship." The holy relationship happens when we undo the unholy or special relationship by shifting the goal of guilt to the goal of forgiveness. In the holy relationship we are guided together to transcend the ego. After having separated for a year and done our own work, we felt more complete and ready for a fulfilling romantic relationship. The *Course* teaches that in the holy relationship, *"Each one has looked within, and seen no lack. Accepting his completion, he would extend it by joining with another, whole as himself."* Though neither of us was fully healed, we were much more whole than ever before. In the relationship's first incarnation, we were two incomplete people coming together in an attempt to become whole. That clearly didn't work. This time around we were guided back together to further transcend the separateness of the ego and step into our holy relationship.

The *Course* teaches: *"The holy relationship, a major step toward the perception of the real world, is learned. It is the old, unholy relationship, transformed and seen anew. The holy re-lationship is a phenomenal teaching accomplishment. In all its aspects, as it begins, develops and becomes accomplished, it rep-resents the reversal of the unholy relationship. Be comforted in this; the only difficult phase is the beginning. For here, the goal of the relationship is abruptly shifted to the exact opposite of what it was."*

This new incarnation of the relationship offered me the opportunity to let go of past resentments, enjoy each moment, and welcome all the new learning that comes with holy love.

Invisible Force

Spirit is the ultimate matchmaker. Whether we realize it or not, we're always being guided in and out of relationships in order to experience the good, the bad, and sometimes the super ugly. When we follow this guidance and allow our ~*ing* to take the lead, we can heal and grow so that we're ready to experience holy love. As soon as my former boyfriend and I came back together through forgiveness, I felt spirit intervene like an invisible driving force. Now our relation-ship was based on acceptance and forgiveness, and there-fore it was holding space for spirit to be present.

Don't get me wrong. Every day wasn't rainbows and butterflies. The fact that our relationship carried old baggage made it the perfect assignment at the time. It was exactly what I needed in order to put my *Course* tools to work and get closer to knowing holy love. I spent plenty of hours ruminating on fearful thoughts. But the miracle was that I was only a head case for a few hours rather than several months. Now I had the necessary tools to combat fear, release the separation, and return to love. This relationship offered me the ideal opportunity to strengthen my spiritual practice even more.

I was ready, willing, and able to show up for this new assignment. But I knew I faced a challenge: because things were going so well, my ego amped up its game, reaching for thoughts of infidelity and lingering bitterness. My ego literally took fears that did not exist before and tried to pummel me with them. For instance, I couldn't shake the ego thought that my boyfriend was going to find a woman whom he liked more than me. This fear was based on our relationship's old form. My ego was dragging my past neuroses into the present. None of it was real. I had two choices: I could choose fear and sabotage my relationship, or I could laugh. The *Course* teaches us not to take the ego and its world seriously, for this makes fear real in our minds. Instead we are urged to laugh gently at the ego's "tiny mad idea" and all its seeming terror. By laughing gently at these mad ideas, I was able to release them one by one. Each time I released an ego thought, I developed a stronger tie to the holiness of the relationship.

While I laughed at the ego, I bolstered my practice by calling on forgiveness as the primary tool for maintaining my holy love and releasing the ego's fear. I prayed daily to let go of the past and forgive the ego's illusions. Through forgiveness I reminded myself of the ego's falseness. I also enlisted the help of a visual reminder by keeping a photo of the two of us on my desk with a Post-it that read, "I release all fear and I know we're being guided." I recited a daily mantra: "I forgive you and release you." And I blessed him each morning before I began my day. I'd say a silent prayer asking spirit to surround him with love and help me release any ego thoughts about our relationship. This daily surrender kept me connected to love and protected the relationship from ego backlash.

Whenever my ego would attack him with fear-based illusions from the past, or flip out about the future, I'd call on forgiveness, release the thought, and start over. Rather than attack, I forgave him, forgave myself, and forgave the thought. Forgiveness became my automatic reset button, which kept me in a state of equilibrium. Because I was so conscious of maintaining the flow of love, spirit continued to be very present within the relationship. Plenty of assignments came my way, but they always led to positive outcomes. For instance, I'd often find myself digging up past fears, such as "I'm not good enough," and "He's going to leave me." In the past, I would've taken out those fears on him or let my mind concoct dark scenarios. This time I turned to my *Course* work for guidance. I'd witness the ego's "tiny mad idea" and recognize it as a fear from the past. Then I'd shine light on how I'd made him special and better than me by seeking completion in the relationship. Finally, I would forgive him and myself. This practice of forgiveness released the illusion that he was separate and immediately restored my connection to spirit and the belief that he and I were one. I worked hard, but I was fully supported by my spirit connection.

Practicing forgiveness was not the only method I used to maintain loving flow: my meditation practice was instrumental as well. I often practiced the "Great Rays Meditation" that had brought me solace in the past. This was the meditation in which I held an image of him and me together and created a vision of light extending from his heart to mine. Through my breath this light expanded until it took over our bodies, transforming us into great rays of light. Practicing this meditation was a powerful reminder that when spirit intervenes, fear can melt away. Love is all that's left.

Releasing Symbols and Specialness

The new incarnation of this relationship offered me optimal opportunities for serious *Course* work. I was challenged to truly release all specialness that I'd placed on the relationship. The *Course* teaches us that the ego's primary focus is on form and symbols. Projections take a range of forms: "He doesn't make enough money," or "Why hasn't he proposed?" or "She doesn't share my religion." The *Course* teaches, *"When you decide on the form of what you want, you lose the understanding of its purpose."* The work in this case is to shift our focus from the form of the relationship to the purpose, which is love. When our primary focus is love, we can release our outside symbols and reconnect with truth. We let go of all the baggage our ego has placed upon it. In my case the practice of forgiveness was guiding me to release all attempts at specialness and attachment to form. When we detach from the form of the ego, we remember that everyone is one. There is no separation and there is no "special love."

The *Course* teaches, *"When we put form, symbols and specialness before purpose we lose our truth."* Another powerful way to release these symbols is to welcome love and inspiration from all areas of life rather than from just one special partner.

I had the opportunity to experience a tremendous amount of love and release of specialness when I went on my book tour. I left town for more than a month. This time away from my relationship could have really set off my ego, getting me into a super needy zone by rousing my fears of losing him. But I did just the opposite. I focused on the love of my life rather than the form. I released the need to perceive my relationship as my only source of love and inspiration. In doing so, I opened the floodgates to receive inspiration and love from every person I came into contact with. While on the road, I spent time with hundreds of women. Women throughout the country were showing up to hear me speak. In each new city I bunked with friends. It was like I was on a month-long slumber party. The love I experienced while on the road filled me up. The ego couldn't thrive, couldn't even survive, in my completeness. Therefore I never felt needy or skittish while away from my boyfriend. We missed each other, but never felt any lack. I was inspired, taken care of, and complete, no matter where I was or who I was with.

I also had the opportunity to enjoy the fiery sparks within my friendships. I spent hours laughing and celebrating life with incredibly inspired women. I felt a sisterhood I'd never known before. By letting go of my grip on the romantic relationship, I was able to truly experience others.

Holy Encounters

The *Course* compares our ego's separation to the idea of sunbeams being separate from the sun, or waves being separate from the ocean. Just as a sunbeam can't separate itself from the sun, and a wave can't separate itself from the ocean, we can't separate ourselves from one another. We are all composed of the same beams of love and are part of the sea of truth. The way to begin to understand this truth is to understand that all encounters are holy encounters. Each person we come in contact with offers us a divine assignment to see love or fear. When we make it our commitment to see love in all relationships, we begin to release the separation and find holiness in all. By choosing to see love in all people I came in contact with, I was able to truly release my ego's separate thoughts. Witnessing these holy encounters of love guided me to release my boyfriend one loving encounter at a time. When I could see love in everyone, I no longer needed it from one special person. There was no separate love.

Mirror

This relationship was also the perfect mirror for me to continue to spot-check my lingering shortcomings. One particular ego thought I still battled was the need to make myself seem special. This issue came up a lot in my relationship. Whenever I'd talk about myself too much or change the conversation to focus on me, my boyfriend would call me out. At first I reacted defensively—but then I turned to my ~ing for help. I used the tool of the universal mirror. The *Course* teaches, *"Perception is a mirror, not a fact. And what I look on is my state of mind, reflected outward."* I

215

learned through this message that the outside world was reflecting my internal state. My discomfort around his response to my perceived specialness reflected my own disgust with my behavior. He mirrored back to me what I needed to work on. This mirror image was a guide to stop defending and start changing my patterns. I took his mirror as a cue to get to work on releasing my special self. Each time I'd have the urge to make myself special, I would say a silent prayer and ask for it to be released. This was really tough at first. It's hard not to get defensive when someone calls you out on your shit, but I worked with the *Course* lesson not to defend against the illusion. If I defended myself, I was strengthening the ego. Instead I looked directly at the ego's behavior, forgave myself, and asked spirit to guide my change. Difficult as it was for me to change this pattern, doing so greatly enhanced my spiritual connection and all my relationships. In this way, my relationship guided me to become more complete.

Gratitude

As I connected with spirit to forgive, embrace holy encounters, and release symbols and specialness, I also practiced gratitude and appreciation. Focusing on gratitude unleashes the love that lives within us and blasts light on the ego. When my ego would try to take me down with fear talk, I'd shine light by concentrating on everything I was grateful for in my relationship. I was pulled up with gratitude rather than dragged down to wallow in feelings of lack. And I didn't limit my gratitude to my romantic relationship; I focused on why I was grateful for all my relationships. This really helped me "de-special" my romantic relationship. I made it a point to reach out to my family and friends and acknowledge how much I loved them. When I looked at my friends and family with gratitude and appreciation, I was able to see my romantic partner as equal to them. This strengthened the wholeness of the relationship and dismantled any residual special form. Furthermore, appreciating him created more abundance within the relationship. Love breeds more love.

Truth

We had each kept our own side of the street clean. We made a commitment to each other to bring all our dark illusions into the light by outing our egos whenever necessary. Therefore, our holy relationship continued to maintain its flow. We spoke up when things were off, and we forgave when necessary. This daily dance of love was everything I could ask for in a relationship. Most important, my fears were truly separate from me now. When old fearful thoughts came up, I immediately saw them as false. They no longer had a hold on me. I could witness the thought, forgive it, and let it go within seconds. This was a miracle. I was now connected to a truthful faith in love.

Spreading the Love

Now that I was serene in my relationship, I was able to revel in the good stuff. I no longer wasted hours and days mired in codependent fear and attack thoughts. This holy love invigorated me. I had abundant time and energy and could share it with the world around me. One amazing effect of being so chilled-out in my holy relationship was that I could show up for my coaching sessions and lectures in a powerful way. Had I been in a tripped-out mindset about my relationship, I never could have served with this type of truth. I would have been focused on my own ego crap and disconnected from the service of spreading the *~ing*. Instead I was able to show up fully, with a clear head and an open connection to everyone around me.

What's more, I was truly able to witness my brotherly relationships become more romantic and my romantic relationship more brotherly. This *Course* lesson, which I introduced in chapter 9, was apparent and tangible. Once again, I was filled with ladylove and all the awesomeness that goes with it. My female friendships became so awesome that I stopped *needing* all my fiery sparks to come from my romantic partner—*all* my relationships fired me up. I was feeling equality in my relationships for the first time. I had released much of the "specialness" I'd created, and therefore was able to spread the love. I now savored the time with my girlfriends equally with the time I spent with my boyfriend.

Becoming Whole

Holy love is available to all of us. However, the goal is *not* to search for the holy relationship. Rather, the goal is to release the blocks to our own wholeness. As the *Course* teaches, *"Your task is not to seek for love, but merely to seek and find all the barriers within yourself that you have built against it."* When we find those barriers and release the blocks, we become whole. By becoming whole, we will attract our likeness. When we no longer need someone else to complete us, we are ready for holy love. Therefore the work in this chapter is designed to further deepen your connection to spirit and guide you to become more whole. Spirit will take care of the rest.

Even though this work is dedicated to your own personal wholeness, we will welcome all relationships into the practice, remembering that relationships are spirit's primary teaching mechanism. Therefore, begin by looking closely at all the relationships in your life, and identify the ways in which they have been your guides.

STEP 1. HOW HAVE YOU INVESTED IN THE ILLUSION?

Remember that the *Course* teaches, *"Insistence means investment."* Therefore, what we insist on focusing on, we're actually investing in. I encourage you in this step to witness what you've been investing in. In what relationships are you reactivating the illusion? The goal of this step is to witness where you're activating more fear by insisting on focusing on it. When we recognize these patterns, we can insist on investing in love instead. For instance, had I insisted on investing in my old illusion that I wasn't good enough for my relationship, I'd have destroyed my opportunity for holy love. By focusing on the good stuff, I chose to insist on love—and therefore invest in love.

STEP 2. WHO ARE YOUR MIRRORS?

The *Course* teaches, *"The world is only in the mind of its maker. Do not believe it is outside of yourself."* Take in this concept. The work in this step will help you further recognize how you've projected your own fear onto others. To get you closer to your own wholeness, it's time to stop pointing the finger at others and turn inward for guidance. Whenever someone rouses you, don't get angry and attack. If you attack, you only reinforce the fear. Instead, ask yourself, *What is coming up for me?* Then invite spirit in to guide you to understand your own ego block. This step is crucial to deepening our wholeness. We must use the mirror to look within for what we cannot find outside ourselves.

STEP 3. CHOOSE TO SEE NO LACK

Remember that the lack you see in others creates more lack in you. The *Course* teaches, *"Sin is a strictly individual perception, seen in the other yet believed by each to be within himself."* Take this step to understand that the sin you see in others reinforces the darkness you see in yourself. Through forgiveness you can weaken this darkness. Once again, strengthen your forgiveness practice by choosing to perceive love rather than darkness. Step by step, choose to perceive joy and love in the darkest spaces. We're not beholden to a mindset or a fear. No matter how big or stubborn it is, we can choose to see it differently. You can use your prayer practice to help guide you, and turn to the forgiveness meditation for further release. Through this work we actually can choose to perceive ourselves differently. We're not beholden to a mindset or a fear, no matter how big or stubborn it is.

Releasing Meditation

(Follow my lead. You can also download this
audio meditation from www.gabbyb.tv/meditate.)

Sit up straight in your chair, with your feet planted
firmly on the ground.

Breathe in through your nose and out through
your mouth. Hold an image in your mind of the
person or people you need to forgive.

Breathe in: I choose to see you without lack.

Breathe out: I choose to see you as love.

Breathe in: I release all fearful projections.

Breathe out: I remember that only love is real.

Breathe in: I call on forgiveness to heal.

Breathe out: I ask for release.

Breathe in: I see you as love.

Breathe out: I see me as love.

Take one last deep breath in and release. When
you're ready, open your eyes to the room.

STEP 4. LET SPIRIT INTERVENE

The *Course* reminds us that the holy relationship, *"a light far brighter than the sun that lights the sky,"* is chosen by spirit as a plan for our reconnection with love. We can now rest easy knowing that we don't need to push, manipulate, or control the outcome. All we have to do is forgive and choose to see love. Through our forgiveness practice we will continue to invite spirit in to take the lead. The *Course* reminds us, *"Every mistake you and your brother make, the other will gently have corrected for you."* Spirit ("the other") will never fail to guide the relationship to holy bliss. You need not do anything. Just let spirit do her thing.

Inviting spirit into your relationships will give you a sense of empowerment. You will no longer feel as though you need to know the how, why, and when. Instead you can relax, knowing that spirit has a rockin' plan. The more we turn over our relationships and desires to the care of our inner guide, the more peaceful our lives become. You'll learn in the coming chapter just how powerful this shift can be.

11

Expect Miracles

Miracles are natural. When they do not occur,

something has gone wrong.

—A COURSE IN MIRACLES

• ◆ •

For nearly a year I was on spiritual cruise control. Everything was jamming. I experienced many miracles and grew to expect them—my commitment to love and spirit had me totally hooked up. I knew the Universe had my back; as my inner life expanded, my ego became tame and my outer life began to mirror the abundance I felt inside. Life was great: my boyfriend and I manifested the home of our dreams; I was working on many new professional projects, lecturing throughout the country; and I'd become respected in my field. There was absolutely nothing wrong. Then, dependably, the ego crept back in. My ego decided to second-guess all the greatness, convincing me it was too good to be true. As a result, I started judging others and attacking myself. Specialness was at an all-time high. My old controlling fears even began to sabotage my miracle-mindedness. In short, my ego freaked out.

Everything was all fine and good when my accomplishments were within the realm of what my ego found reasonable. But the moment my internal and external states hit a higher plane, my ego karate-chopped my spiritual flow.

Hooking into these fear-based thoughts lowered my energy and weakened my connection to spirit. I'd moved into a funky space and disconnected from the loving presence of my inner guide. I was now dealing with thoughts like "You can't have it this easy. Something is bound to go wrong." These thoughts could take me down, lower my energy, and disturb my flow.

My thoughts informed my energy, and my energy informed my experiences. I saw how my low-level thoughts of disbelief weakened my connection to spirit, thereby attracting old chaotic patterns and negative outcomes. Each time I'd get hooked into the thought that "this is too good to be true," I'd start second-guessing situations and feel fearful and unconfident. These feelings of inadequacy and unworthiness created more negativity. In this negative state I struggled to do good work, flailed about in my relationships, and felt my overall sense of peace slam out of balance. Considering that this pattern stemmed from my own mind, there seemed to be a simple solution: *Just keep my thoughts positive and life will flow again.* But it wasn't all that easy. I'd rev up my *Course* work and get connected back to my ~ing. This would work for a while, but my ego was determined to take me down. Ego had rocked out the nastiest trick of all: fear of greatness.

But I had an advantage over my ego and was able to resist its backlash. I turned inward for help and asked for guidance, knowing spirit would have a solution. In a meditation

I waited for a response. Coming out of my meditation I felt the intuition to walk over to my bookshelf. My hand passed over the shelf and landed on Marianne Williamson's book *A Return to Love*. I smiled and welcomed the guidance. I opened the book to a page that had been dog-eared. Then I laughed upon realizing what I'd been guided to read. The page I turned to featured Marianne's most famous quote:

Our deepest fear is not that we are inadequate. Our deepest fear is that we are powerful beyond measure. It is our light, not our darkness, that most frightens us. We ask ourselves, Who am I to be brilliant, gorgeous, talented, fabulous? Actually, who are you not to be? You are a child of God. Your playing small does not serve the world. There is nothing enlightened about shrinking so that other people won't feel insecure around you. We are all meant to shine, as children do. We were born to make manifest the glory of God that is within us. It's not just in some of us; it's in everyone. And as we let our own light shine, we unconsciously give other people permission to do the same. As we are liberated from our own fear, our presence automatically liberates others.

That said it all. I could not deny this spirit ~ingTervention. In that moment spirit worked through the text to bring me back to equilibrium. Marianne's words reminded me that accepting my greatness was not something to shy away from. Greatness is our birthright and our truth. Rather than hide from miracles, it was my duty to embrace them. By shining brightly on the world, I could ignite light in others. Her words inspired me to keep it simple and, once again, surrender to my inner guide.

Back to Basics

In order to reclaim my spirit mojo, I had to get back to basics. I revisited my early *Course* work, checking back in with the ego's nasty tricks. Yet again I became the witness to the ego's fear in order to disconnect from the negativity. In the midst of this ego flare-up, I experienced many Holy Instants. I now had the strength of my spirit connection to help me immediately recognize those feelings and thoughts as the ego's tricks.

Rather than freak out and let my ego rain on my awesome life parade, I chose to pray. I prayed, *Inner guide, please enter into my mind and take the steering wheel. I am committed to love and miracles. Keep me in the flow.*

The loving response I heard time and time again was this: *You're right where you need to be. Accept all this greatness. Embrace it!* These ~*ing* reminders would tranquilize the ego and guide me back to love. Some days I'd call on my ~*ing* several times for these gentle reminders. These spirit ~*ing*Terventions also came in other forms. I often heard the voice of my coach, Rha Goddess, in the back of my mind. Her mantra was, "Let the world show up for the party that is you." I also wore a reminder around my neck in the form of a necklace I'd received from Marianne Williamson. It was a scroll pendant on a chain. Inside the scroll was her famous quote, the one that had reignited my ~*ing*.

The Universe Wants Us to Be Happy

Our ego works overtime to convince us that happiness comes with a price tag. Western cultures in particular have an overarching ego belief system that we have to struggle to "get there." The ego convinces us that pain has a purpose. Suffering, struggle, and pain are necessary to keep the ego alive and separate us from love. That's why my ego flipped out when things got good. When miracles began to flow naturally, my ego reminded me of pain, convincing me to think things were too good to be true. Even in the midst of my commitment to *Course* work, ego trapped me in the belief of pain to keep me small. This was what led me to second-guess the effortless flow of miracles.

Once I recognized this pattern, I committed to saying no to the ego's playing small. I had to weaken the false idea that pain has a purpose or that we have to struggle to be happy. I remembered that as long as I had faith in spirit, miracles would occur naturally. It's not that I sat on a meditation pillow all day long, expecting miracles to occur spontaneously. Rather, I stayed connected to my ~ing and took spiritually aligned action instead of succumbing to the ego's pushy and controlling approach to life. Since my primary goal was to stay connected to spirit, everything else flowed. Each outward action I took was backed by strong intuition and inspiration. All I needed to do was commit to the belief that with spirit as my guide, anything was possible.

Turning It Over

By this point in my *Course* study, I was practicing the third section of the book, which is the *Manual for Teachers*. The work in this section prepares the *Course* student to become a spiritual teacher. The lessons are powerful and consistently lead us to turn to our inner guides for complete healing. We are urged to invite spirit in to continue guiding us to become teachers in our own right.

There is a section in the *Manual for Teachers* titled "How Is Correction Made?" This section was profound for me. What resonated with me most was the guidance that in order to heal, it would be essential for me to let all my own mistakes be corrected by my ~ing. The *Course* teaches: *"If he senses even the faintest hint of irritation in himself as he responds to anyone, let him instantly realize that he has made an interpretation that is not true. Then let him turn within to his eternal Guide, and let Him judge what the response should be."*

This lesson led me to realize that even as I became the teacher, I still had to remain humble to my eternal guide. I would always be watched over as I continued to practice the principles of love. Even once I fully stepped into the role of teacher, I'd still be a student.

As I transitioned into the role of teacher, I also accepted that all my obstacles were opportunities. I welcomed each attack thought or difficult situation as an opportunity to grow spiritually. This helped me accept the great things that were happening around me because I was no longer fearful of something going wrong. I wholly accepted that a changed plan or altered course meant that something better was on the way. I was capable of living in each moment, accepting greatness and change as equally valuable components of my spiritual journey. In honoring this truth I reactivated my spiritual mojo and began flowing with life once again.

Already "There"

For most of my life I lived with the belief that I was working toward some special place or trying to attain some elite status. This theory was based on a way of thinking that is familiar to many people: that a certain level of success, a certain type of boyfriend, or a hefty bank balance will magically confer happiness upon us. I came to understand that true happiness comes from the exact opposite place. The *Course* taught me that regardless of my outside experience, happiness was my only function. Finally I understood that there was no special status or perfect relationship or amount of money that could complete me. I had "it" all along. Even though I didn't realize it at the time, peace of mind was all I was seeking. Learning to access my inner state of peace is by far my greatest accomplishment.

Accepting Right-Mindedness

Accepting happiness as my only function was a major step in fully committing to the *Course's* true perception. Upon recognizing this, I reflected on all the ways in which spirit had worked through me to guide me back to inner peace and joy. I thought back to my most desperate moments of drug addiction and most torturous romantic struggles, and considered how all those experiences were necessary tools for my spiritual growth. My ~*ing* had been working tirelessly all this time. I could now look fondly on my past with gratitude for all the learning and healing I'd undergone. The *Course* says, *"What could you not accept, if you but knew that everything that happens, all events, past, present, and to come, are gently planned by One Whose only purpose is your good?"* It was now clear that all my life's experiences were

233

gently guided by spirit. All I needed to do was stay willing, perceive happiness as my only function, and allow spirit to intervene.

By fully turning my belief system over to the care of my ~*ing*, I now perceived miracles as natural. This faith in miracles raised my levels of happiness and peace, thereby raising my awareness of the miracle. I felt the presence of spirit in each new encounter, knowing I'd been guided to that specific person for an opportunity to learn and spread love. I had faith in miracles and expected them.

Maintaining the Vibration

Having faith in miracles was a belief system I needed to consciously maintain. It's easy to get taken out by the ego— even when you're a miracle-minded lady. Anything from a rude person to PMS could knock me out of spiritual alignment. Knowing this, I made it my goal to stay connected to spirit no matter what. I used daily reinforcement to stay focused on the good stuff. I made reminders for myself in my phone and computer calendars. These reminders would pop up throughout the day in the form of messages such as "*I accept happiness now*," or "*I expect miracles*." These simple notes guided me back to spirit and helped me choose happiness time and time again.

Furthermore, my spiritual consciousness allowed me to

witness the Universe reminding me to stay in flow. Often these reminders would show up in seemingly unlikely places. I found loving quotes written on bathroom stalls, read inspiring messages posted on blogs or Internet boards, and heard beautiful music from inside windows as I passed by on the sidewalk. Each of these reminders reignited spirit's love and gently reminded me that spirit had my back.

Another way of maintaining my spiritual flow was to keep an eye on the ego at all times. Through my own experience and the experiences of others, I had seen time and again how crafty the ego could be. For instance, a client of mine came to me full of fear. She explained how great her life had become as a result of her spiritual practice. Her relationships, career, and overall sense of peace were flowing naturally. However, she felt a tremendous sense of fear that she just couldn't shake. She kept repeating, "Will I survive this?" I laughed when I realized what was going on. I responded, "You will survive, but your ego won't." This is a powerful example of how the ego will try to take us down when things get good. The ego cannot survive in our peaceful state. Therefore we will feel as though we cannot survive, because we've functioned for so long believing that we *are* the ego. Knowing that *you are not your ego* will help you stay connected to love. To keep my spiritual flow going, I make a daily practice of reminding myself that I am not my ego and that it's okay if my ego doesn't survive.

In order to fully maintain my faith in spirit, I had to

give up some lingering habits. One in particular was gossip. This was a tough one: my ego had ingrained this pattern in me for more than twenty years. But by this point I was way too into love and miracles to lower my inner vibration through gossip. Anytime I found myself tempted to talk about someone, I'd immediately shift the conversation. Gossip no longer served me—it felt funky. Spirit guided me to become conscious of the pattern so I could maintain my commitment to happiness and miracles. Listening to my inner guide kept my vibration high.

Thoughts Merging with Love

Over time my thoughts merged with love. I instinctively chose love on a moment-to-moment basis, thereby becoming one with my internal guide. This connection helped me focus on love in every corner of my life. I found love in a hot cup of coffee and a miracle in a smile from a stranger. My love radar was on high. It was as if the voice of my ~*ing* had become my voice. I was no longer leaning on my ~*ing* as a mentor. I'd become my own mentor. The *Course* says that our internal guide is always with us, even when we no longer rely on its guidance. Our ~*ing* is referred to as a friend who lives inside and is one with us.

I felt this oneness and fully embraced it. With each breath I felt spirit come through and heighten my loving perception. I had turned inward to connect with the wise and thoughtful part of my soul, the part of me that remembered why I was here in this world at this time—the part of me that remembered where I came from and where I was going. I looked on my past fondly, honoring my journey. Through my prayer and meditation I connected to the little girl inside me who had fearlessly faced her inner demons and transcended the darkness. This little girl represented the voice of all those who'd disconnected from their spirit at one point in time. I had rejoined with my spirit self. I had reconnected with my past, present, and future. This connection allowed spirit to fully move through me so that I could serve at my highest capacity. It was time for me to help others retrieve their connections, too.

Extending Healing to Others

Accepting my own healing and right-mindedness led me to directly and automatically extend healing to others. I had to accept my own healing before I could fully extend it. As the *Course* says, *"For you must have before you can give."* This acceptance is the sole responsibility of what the *Course* refers to as the "miracle worker." The *Course* teaches: *"By denying your mind any destructive potential and reinstating its purely constructive powers, you place yourself in a position to undo the level of confusion of others."*

Now that my constructive powers were restored and I was at peace, I could extend that peace to others. For instance, upon entering a room I could feel the energy shift when I was connected to spirit. I could intend to share light with the room, and the overall presence of the people in the space would shift accordingly.

This type of energy exchange became very powerful in all of life's circumstances, from the small (getting into a cab with an impatient driver) to the potentially unnerving (standing in front of an audience of strangers). Bringing my healing presence in all scenarios greatly boosted the energetic state of those around me. It was incredible to watch the energy shift as I intended it to. By simply saying a silent prayer and choosing always to be of service with my thoughts and energy, I was able to transform those around me. Therefore, other people's issues no longer tripped me up. I stopped feeling responsible for saving people; I understood that I could best help them by maintaining my own miracle-minded way of being. Accepting my own peace was the greatest gift I could offer the world.

Becoming a Miracle Worker

The *Course* teaches that miracles are expressions of love. When we become miracle-minded (or right-minded) we express love naturally and, as a consequence, perform miracles. Our mind creates our reality, so miracle-minded thoughts create miraculous outcomes. My commitment to love and miracles was preparing me to be a miracle worker. The *Course* teaches, *"Before miracle workers are ready to undertake their function in this world, it is essential that they fully understand the fear of release."*

The fear of release was what I had struggled with before I was able to accept miracles. When I doubted the miracles of my life, I hooked back into the ego's thinking that I was a separate body that could be harmed and that all the awesomeness was *too good to be true.* In retrospect I understand why this freak-out occurred. My ego was trying a final, desperate tactic to hold me back from becoming a miracle worker. The ego was afraid of releasing my perception of littleness and embracing the magnitude of a miracle worker. But spirit was committed to teaching me the truth and guiding me back to love and miracles. I was reminded that my fear was a construct of my ego and not part of the truthful spiritual mindset that I'd grown to believe in. By accepting this miracle-minded way of being, I was now prepared to become a miracle worker.

Accepting Happiness as Your Only Function

To fully understand the function of a miracle worker, it is imperative that we embrace happiness as our only function.

This is a difficult step for most, owing to the ego's belief in pain and purpose. Believing in our limited capacity is what keeps us small. Regardless of how far we've come down the spiritual path, fear still lurks in the shadows, in one form or another.

At this point in your journey it's time for you to accept your greatness and welcome miracles. Becoming a miracle worker requires your full trust in the miracle-minded belief system of love. The exercises in this chapter are dedicated to accepting happiness as your only function. I'll guide you to witness when you're resisting love and miracles. Then I'll lead you to immediately invite your ~*ing* to intervene. Finally, I'll lead you to deepen and solidify the reconditioning process by reinforcing the daily belief that happiness is your only function. This step in the process is crucial to becoming a teacher of love. We must have faith in miracles if we're to become miracle workers.

STEP 1. HOW DO YOU DENY LOVE AND MIRACLES?

I'll preface this step by acknowledging that it's very likely that your ego resists miracles at all costs. Many of my coaching clients will get deeply into the miracle mindset, only to begin denying it as time passes. They'll stop meditating, praying, and forgiving, and cave in to the ego's faith in fear. This is totally natural if you're not fully committed to happiness and peace. We have to remember that no matter how committed we are to love, the ego is equally, if not more, committed to fear. Therefore we must be honest about how our ego plays tricks, convincing us to deny miracles. Ask yourself, "How does my ego deny miracles?" ~*ing*-write for ten minutes on this topic and let your truth come to the page.

STEP 2. LET GO OF LITTLENESS

Think about how often you find yourself lowering your expectations in an attempt to insulate yourself against disappointment. This is typical in our society. We are often warned against getting our hopes up for fear of failure. This is the opposite of miracle-minded thinking. In these cases the ego is once again protecting itself by playing small and hiding from great potential. The best way out of this ego trick is to reconnect with spirit by reminding yourself that whatever you desire is on its way—that, or something better. If you find yourself lowering your expectations, begin a prayer practice of inviting spirit to remind you that you're supported. Say out loud, "I know spirit has my back. I know I'm being guided to this or something better. Show me what you've got." Through this prayer you'll reconnect with the truth that the Universe is fully supporting you at all times. Fear of failure is unnecessary.

STEP 3. ASK YOUR ~*ing* TO GUIDE YOU BACK TO LOVE

As you know by now, the solution to any fear-based problem lives in the spiritual perception of your inner guide. Upon looking at this inventory of ego sabotage, once again invite your ~*ing* in for healing. Whenever you witness your ego denying miracles, ask your ~*ing* to intervene and remind you of your true perception: faith in love. To further aid in the process, you may want to leave yourself gentle reminders to choose love over fear. For instance, I have a framed print in my office that says *Only Love Is Real*. I look at it often and remember my truth. I am catapulted back into my miracle-mindedness. Leave yourself notes, Black-Berry or iPhone reminders, and calendar updates that say "I expect miracles." Work with your inner guide to commit fully to your right mind.

STEP 4. REINFORCE HAPPINESS AS YOUR ONLY FUNCTION

This happy reinforcement comes in many forms. For example, when I chose to stop gossiping, I ignited more happiness in my life. By making the conscious decision to end an old ego pattern and choose love instead, I poured light onto the ego and became more miracle-minded. I encourage you to find ways to further strengthen your love practice. Make forgiveness your primary goal in all relationships. Welcome miracles into your life and pay attention to them. See love in all people, objects, and situations. You can see love in an orange-leafed October tree, an acquaintance you bump into on the street, or a cup of steaming black tea. *Choose* to see love. *Expect* miracles.

Continue to remind yourself daily that happiness is your only function. Know that the ego will combat this each waking moment, and know that it is our job as miracle workers to bleed love. Be gentle with yourself. This isn't a new opportunity to beat yourself up every time you deny a miracle. Just stay committed and let your ~*ing* continue to guide you back to happiness.

STEP 5. PRACTICE DEFENSELESSNESS

As my inner light grew brighter, certain resisters appeared, attempting to snuff out that light. One person in particular really hooked into my energy field. This person was very stuck in her ego, which led her to attack me tirelessly for no good reason. At first my ego's response was to defend against her wrongful attacks. That didn't work. By this point in my spiritual journey, that type of ego-driven response made me feel worse. Attacking against someone else's attack created more negativity. So, rather than defensively attack back, my inner guide reminded me of a *Course* lesson: "*In my defenselessness my safety lies.*" In order to maintain my miracle-mindedness I had to stick to the *Course*'s plan and practice true defenselessness. This was not easy at first, but I took it one day at a time. To help guide me along my path I thought about enlightened masters such as Jesus and Gandhi. In the midst of an attack I'd ask spirit, *What would Gandhi do?* Each attack became a new opportunity to channel my inner Gandhi and focus on defenselessness. Spirit guided me through prayer to see this person as an equal, and through meditation I cut the energetic cords between us. These exercises required daily commitment and became powerful tools that strengthened my spiritual growth.

Defensiveness will lower your miracle-mindedness and spiritual power. Practicing defenselessness is imperative to a powerful spiritual practice because it keeps you connected to love. When you defend, you fuel more attack and anger into your life and out onto the world. Begin your practice of defenselessness by recognizing whom you are defending against. Then say a prayer: *In my defenselessness my safety lies.* Finally, choose to cut the energetic cord between you and your attacker. The following meditation will be your guide.

Cord-Cutting Meditation

(For the audio version, visit www.gabbyb.tv/meditate.)

Sit up straight in your chair.

Take a deep breath in through your nose and out through your mouth.

Think of the person who has attacked you.

Identify the area in your body where you're energetically affected by this attack.

Breathe deeply into that space in your body.

On the exhale, release.

In your mind's eye, invite this person's image into your meditation.

The person is standing before you.

Envision a thick black cord connecting you both.

This cord represents the negative energetic connection that is keeping you connected to your ego's fear.

Commit in this moment to cut the cord.

Breathe in: I surrender my will and attack. I welcome the cord to be cut.

Envision Gandhi, Jesus, or any enlightened master with a large sword.

Welcome them to cut the cord.

See the cord fall to the ground.

Breathe out release.

Know that the energetic cord has been cut.

Welcome a feeling of release to pass over you.

Say a prayer for the other person: "May you be
happy, healthy, and free. May you live with
ease."

STEP 6. FORGIVE YOUR EGO

The ego will do everything in its power to block us from
miracles. Now that you're in the practice of consciously
choosing miracles and turning to love for help, the ego will
rev up its game. As the *Course* says, *"The ego is likely to
attack when you react lovingly, because it has evaluated you
as unloving and you are going against its judgment. The ego
will attack your motives as soon as they become clearly out
of accord with its perception. It is surely pointless to attack in
return."* As you become more miracle-minded, the ego will
work harder. Therefore it is important to stay highly conscious of the ego's nasty tricks. Combating this ego back-

lash is quite simple: just forgive the ego and forgive yourself. Through forgiveness you will remember the ego's falseness and be catapulted back to love.

The upcoming chapter will help you reinforce your miracle mindset even more. The true purpose of the miracle is to be love and share love. Therefore it is your job at this time to focus on welcoming love and happiness as your primary function so that you, too, can become a miracle worker.

12
Spirit Junkie

Spirit is in a state of grace forever. Your reality
is only spirit. Therefore you are in a state of
grace forever.

—A COURSE IN MIRACLES

• ◆ •

t's pretty trippy to write your own story in chronological order. At some point you're bound to wind up in the now. And here we are, my friends, in the present moment. I've looked forward to this. The now is super cool, and I'm psyched to share the miracle of where my *Course* work has guided me.

So where has my spiritual journey brought me? I've been led to a life beyond my wildest dreams. I went far "out there" into a world I projected, only to turn inward and accept happiness as the only true perception. Through my journey I've been guided back home. Spirit reminded me of who I truly am: a spirit among spirits with the mission to be love and share love. I'm now in a place that the *Course* refers to as the "Happy Dream": a time when miracles become natural and our mind is aligned with love. The Happy Dream is a mindset—a way of experiencing the world through eyes of joy. Today I live in the world, but think with the thoughts of heaven. Having broken through my ego's chains, happiness resurfaced and love is all I choose to see. Living in the Happy Dream doesn't mean I'm an enlightened master detached from the world. I still love bright high heels, soy-milk lattes, and tight jeans that make my butt look good. Today I can love these worldly things, but I don't *need* them to be happy. Happiness is a choice I make, not a hot new purchase, a romantic partner, or a title on a business card. I choose happiness everywhere: on a sunlit sidewalk, on a crowded train, in a hip downtown boutique. But it's not the outward surroundings that make me happy. Happiness is in my mind.

In the Happy Dream I no longer think, *I want it this way.* Instead I pray, *Spirit, show me what you've got.* Offering up my desires to my inner guide detaches me from the outcome and brings me back into the present moment. When I surrender to the fact that there is a plan so much better than mine, I don't have to *go out and get and do, do, do, do.* I can relax, knowing that there is a force inside guiding me to everything I need. Then my work is effortless, my relationships are holy, and I feel complete. Welcoming this way of perceiving life is what the Happy Dream is all about. It's a full-blown surrender, allowing spirit to guide the way. Surrendering allows us to stay present in the moment and release all future expectations. Instead of analyzing our worries, we can relinquish them to the care of spirit for transformation. The *Course* teaches, *"What can frighten me when I let all things be exactly as they are?"* Living in the Happy Dream lets your attachments off the hook, accepting everything as it is. Ego's separation melts away and we feel as though we always have a friend by our side, leading us to miracles. Today in the Happy Dream I'm not yet in heaven, but I am far from hell. Happiness is what I choose. I ask for help and my thoughts turn back to love. This is not an accident and it's not luck: it is the result of my conscientious effort to change the way I think, coupled with a deep desire to believe in miracles.

The Happy Dream is available to us all. We just have to choose for it—which is to say, each of our choices must lead us to it. Choosing the Holy Instant and asking for a miracle is what will bring you back to a happy state of mind. Just keep asking. Early in my *Course* study I read a passage: "*You have little trust in me yet, but it will increase as you turn more and more often to me instead of to your ego for guidance. The result will convince you increasingly that this choice is the only sane one you can make.*" I listened to this passage and continually turned to spirit for help. The more I ask for guidance, the more I believe that it is the only sane choice to make. By adding up all your requests, you, too, will eventually think to ask all the time. Asking will become instinctual. You'll truly understand that all misery is associated with the ego and all joy is associated with spirit. The *Course* teaches that our faith, joined with spirit's understanding, is all we need. And with this relationship to spirit we will *"build a ladder planted in the solid rock of faith, and rising even to heaven."* Continue to choose joy and climb the ladder back to heaven with spirit by your side.

Today I'm a spirit junkie. I feel spirit inform my mind each moment, guiding me to extend love to the world. Lesson 267 from the *Course* describes this feeling perfectly: *"Peace fills my heart, and floods my body with the purpose of forgiveness. Now my mind is healed, and all I need to save the world is given me. Each heartbeat brings me peace; each breath infuses me with strength."* I've learned through my dedication to the *Course* that love is where "it's" at. My focus on love makes anything possible. Combining my fierce desire for love with a full surrender, I live a life beyond my wildest dreams. I never could have imagined this life. In fact, there was a time when I couldn't dream of a day without anxiety and inner terror. But that's all changed. One day at a time I transformed my thoughts, and today I know true peace. Welcoming spirit into each moment allows me to live this truth. My only goal today is peace of mind. When spirit's in the driver's seat, I'm hooked up. As a messenger of miracles I offer my own spiritual connection as a healing mechanism for the world.

For me, the Happy Dream still has plenty of assignments and ego moments. But they're fleeting and come to me for a purpose: to strengthen my faith in miracles. One of the ways I remain in the Happy Dream is to remember that the purpose of living this groovy life is to share the goods. My work now is to extend my faith in miracles to everyone around me. I can share love with my doorman, my Twitter followers, and a stranger on the street. Each encounter is a holy encounter, one that offers me an opportunity to extend peace and love.

Authentic Service

It's one thing to be connected to spirit for your own happiness and inner peace, but accessing spirit to serve the world takes you to a whole new level. As a true spirit junkie I follow the *Course's* guided path to be a miracle worker. The purpose of a miracle worker is to help others shift their perceptions from fear back to love. My faith in the *Course* enables me to work with authentic power to serve at my highest capacity. The woman I am today serves much differently from the woman I once was. Looking back, I can see how much I've grown. My connection to spirit made my service mentality not about *me*, but about *we*. Reflecting on this, I turned inward and asked my ~*ing, How has my service mentality grown?* Spirit answered loud and clear, *Your own healing is healing the world. Now you're an extension of love. You're no longer hiding behind service—instead you're truly serving. You are a miracle worker.* This conversation with my ~*ing* was short, clear, and inarguable.

In becoming spiritually inclined, I've learned that my purpose is to heal the world and that our true job is to be miracle workers, not stockbrokers, publicists, fashion designers, and so on. I now understand that I'm here in this world at this time to heal the perceptions of those around me, thereby healing the world. I realized that in the past I'd hidden behind my outward service actions to avoid confronting my own internal issues. Instead of dealing, I was doing. My actions, though seemingly altruistic, actually had been quite selfish. They were a fabulous way for me to perceive myself as accomplished and selfless while avoiding having to deal with the terror in my mind. I was hiding from my fears by focusing on my "fight" for the rights of others. I focused on my fight for reproductive rights, my fight against violence, and other causes that, though worthy and important, served as personal cover-ups. The fight was my way of justifying the fact that I was running away from the war in my mind.

Ironically, I couldn't support any altruistic mission with the energy it deserved, because I had a spiritual disconnect. At that time, service was a way for me to avoid healing. Ego convinced me that fighting for others made me special, when in reality it furthered the separation and my own healing. Now I can look at my past "fight" and gently laugh. I can smile knowing how far I've come and honor myself for everything I did to survive—even if survival meant hiding behind a fight. Today I no longer need to change the world around me. I just need to change the way I see it.

Today I can show up for the rights of others because I've shown up for me. Now that I've chosen love over fear, I can share miracles and move forward fearlessly. My miracle-mindedness can bleed through every action, every thought. My service to others and to myself are one and the same. I understand that if I'm vibrating at a frequency of love, I am of service. My only function is to be happy. My happiness is contagious.

As a miracle worker I am not immune to anger or attack thoughts, and I cannot hide from them; rather, I turn to spirit for miracles. By choosing the miracle, I feel empowered and therefore can strengthen the energy and thoughts of those around me. I know that if my energy is aligned with faith in miracles, I am supporting more miracles.

I now have direction. I no longer need to figure it all out or know some specific outcome. I can simply invite spirit in to be my guide. As the *Course* says, *"Don't try to purify yourself before coming to me. I am the purifier."* That's what this book is about: letting spirit intervene to heal us in order to become miracle workers who help heal the world. It is our duty to clear the space in our own minds and hearts so that we can take spiritually aligned action. Only then will our actions truly have massive effects.

The Function of the Miracle Worker

The *Course* teaches, *"Miracles are natural. When they do not occur, something has gone wrong."* To become miracle workers, we must believe this statement wholeheartedly and embrace the belief system of miracles. The *Course* teaches that there is no order of difficulty in miracles; therefore, no miracle is more important than another. We cannot control the miracle. I used to ask for *the exact* miracle I wanted: for the guy to call back, the contract to be signed, or the debt to disappear. I've learned that I cannot control the outcome of the miracle; all I can do is allow it to occur. I now know that spirit's plan is much better than mine, and therefore maybe the guy isn't supposed to call back or the contract isn't supposed to be signed. When and how a miracle occurs is not up to us. Our job is simply to maintain our belief in love. As such, anytime we feel out of alignment with love, we must invite spirit to intervene and arrange the miracle. Then we expect it to occur. Our expectation supports the miracle.

As miracle workers we must always respond to wrong-minded thinking with a desire to heal it. The miracle is the denial of the ego and an affirmation of love. By inviting spirit to clean up our ego's thoughts, we shift our perception and choose love over fear. *This is the miracle.* Through our practice of forgiveness and commitment to right-minded thoughts, we support miracles.

Accepting Our Own Healing Is What Heals

The *Course* teaches, *"The miracle worker is generous out of self-interest."* My choice to heal my perceptions has been the catalyst for my own healing. Each time I choose to forgive someone, the relationship is healed and I'm closer to the true miracle-minded perception. If one person is less connected to the miracle, the miracle worker can help deepen that connection merely through her belief system. There is no convincing others of miracles: just believe in them. All I need to do today is believe in miracles and everything works out. I believe that there is a plan greater than mine, and that I am part of the function of a colossal source of love that lives inside each of us. There is nothing separate about my internal love and the love of others, and there is nothing separate from my thoughts. My thoughts are felt and heard by those who don't even know my name. My thoughts affect everything around me. Clearing space for miracles is all I have to do today. Practicing these principles in all my affairs has healed others and me simultaneously. As soon as we invite spirit to change our mind, everyone involved receives a healing. When all we want to see is love, all we see is love.

The Miracle Worker: A Teacher of Love

The *Course* teaches that we all can be miracle workers if we want it. Spirit calls on all of us, but few will answer. The message of this chapter is to inspire you to answer spirit's call—to open your heart to become a miracle worker who shares love through personal healing and growth. If you choose to be a teacher of love, there are several functions you must live by. I love this part of the gig because it's all laid out for us in the *Course's Manual for Teachers*. Following these suggested guidelines I remain humble and connected to my true purpose: love.

Trust

Learning to trust in the power that is in but not of me is crucial to being a miracle worker. I now understand that I'm not a separate self who makes things happen. Instead I am part of an infinite energy source that everyone can access. Choosing to access this source of spiritual power gives me the trust in spirit, not my ego, as my guide. My favorite message from the *Course* is *"Who would attempt to fly with the tiny wings of a sparrow when the mighty power of an eagle has been given him?"* I have faith in my eagle wings and I allow them to guide my direction as a student and as a teacher.

Honesty

Trust in spirit is what guides me to stay honest. My faith in miracles keeps me away from the ego's deceptive thoughts, and I remain connected to love. Honesty keeps my perceptions clean and my actions fueled by love.

Tolerance

The principle of tolerance is all about not judging others. Today I have a daily practice of releasing all judgment. When an attack thought enters into my mind, I pray for it to be transformed. Judgment implies lack of trust and honesty. Judgment lowers my spiritual connection. By committing to release all judgment, I stay connected to the service of being a miracle worker.

Gentleness

As a teacher of love, I know I cannot harm anyone. Harm comes from an inner judgment of others and reflects my own judgment of myself. Harmfulness wipes out my true function of inner peace. Today judgment and harm no longer serve me. In fact, they make me confused, fearful, and angry. Therefore, as a miracle worker I choose against judgment and in turn allow the gentleness of spirit to pass through me. This gentleness is an extension of my inner peace. Living this way makes me feel great. As the *Course* teaches, *"Who chooses hell when he perceives a way to*

Heaven? And who would choose the weakness that must come from harm in place of the unfailing, all-encompassing and limitless strength of gentleness?"

Joy

Joy is inevitable when you're aligned with spirit. Since I've chosen to follow spirit as my guide, I am led to release attack and be gentle. This gentleness always results in joy. When an attack thought comes in, I turn inward for help and immediately reconnect with joy. Why wouldn't I be joyous when love is what I choose?

Defenselessness

When my miracle-mindedness grew stronger, my defenses weakened. I no longer felt like defending myself against the attacks of others. I recognized this as investing in their illusion. When you think with love, you have nothing to defend against. Each day I practice defenselessness to the best of my ability. When I maintain a defenseless attitude and choose to see love in my attacker, I am catapulted into a state of peace. It is imperative that the teacher of love be defenseless. This attribute is a sure sign that your faith lies in miracles rather than in the ego's illusion.

Generosity

The term *generosity* has an awesome meaning to the teacher of love. In this case generosity is based on trust. The miracle worker trusts that giving things away is not a loss but a gain. In the ego's world, the concept of generosity means to give something up. In spirit's perception, it means giving away in order to keep. This is the opposite of what we've been taught by our ego minds. When we as teachers of love are generous out of self-interest, we generously give that which supports our own inner peace.

Patience

When I became certain about my spiritual connection and inner love, I knew the Universe had my back. Therefore I no longer feared the future. This released my ego's need to future-trip and hold on to the past. I forgave the past and accepted that love was guiding me forward. Embracing miracles provided me with certainty and a sense of peace. The *Course* says, *"Those who are certain of the outcome can afford to wait, and wait without anxiety."* Patience is imperative for the teacher of love, for it confirms faith.

Faithfulness

Though I've accepted love as my only function, I still waver from time to time. There are plenty of moments when the ego creeps in, but my faith in spirit always guides me back to love. The more I turn to my faith in spirit, the more faith I have that *only love is real.* The *Course* teaches: *"To give up all problems to one Answer is to reverse the thinking of the world entirely. And that alone is faithfulness. Nothing but that really deserves the name. Yet each degree, however small, is worth achieving. Readiness, as the text notes, is not mastery."*

This concept is awesome. The teacher doesn't need to be a master to teach. All you need is to choose faith in love, and your readiness will lead the way.

Open-Mindedness

Open-mindedness comes with lack of judgment. Just as judgment shuts love down, open-mindedness invites love in. The open-minded can see light where there is darkness and peace where there is pain. Through forgiveness the open-minded are set free from the ego's illusion and catapulted into a state of love.

You Are a Miracle Worker

If you've applied even a fraction of the principles in this book to your own life, you've reactivated your own inner spirit. By applying even one of the tools in this book, you've participated in a miracle. Your simple choice to perceive the world with love produced a miraculous shift. One Holy Instant is all you need to remember where you came from and reconnect with your true purpose, even if only for a moment. My intention for this book is to reignite your spirit, who will guide you back to love. If enough of us get our ~*ing* on we can change the world. My hope is that you carry these tools into your life and stay inspired to know true love. My deep desire was all I needed to restore my faith in love and miracles. If you desire this same faith, you, too, will be guided.

Each moment offers a new opportunity to strengthen our spiritual connection. Below are gentle reminders of ways to keep growing your own relationship with spirit.

STEP 1. REMEMBER "IT" IS IN YOU

In my lectures and workshops I often feel a sense of urgency from the audience. There is an underlying desperation in the room, which is based on the need to find an outside solution to an inside problem. There is a need to "get there." I understand this deeply. The biggest gift I've received is my faith that we're already "there." I hope this book has led you to know that everything you're seeking is already in you and there's no place "out there" to find it. Turn inward and ask for guidance. Undergoing this transformation and restoration often can feel far out of reach. Don't get discouraged. Continue to remind yourself that it isn't far at all. It's in you right now. Remain willing to take the necessary steps to continue turning inward and dealing with the past to clear all blocks to love. The *Course* has taught me that we take care of the future by living in the present.

STEP 2. ALWAYS CHOOSE LOVE

The key to maintaining a loving mindset is to remember that forgiveness is your primary tool. Whenever you're in doubt, throw down the F word, knowing that forgiveness will set you free. Love is experienced to the extent that we believe in love. In order to enjoy our own loving experience, we must commit to keeping our thoughts aligned with love. Therefore, stay connected to love through your forgiveness practice. Remember what the *Course* asks: *"Would you rather be right or happy?"* When happiness is our primary function, we turn to forgiveness as the bridge back to peace. Maintain your loving connection by releasing others. Each time you feel resentment, ask spirit to intervene and transform the thought through forgiveness. By forgiving others I was healed. My own healing is now a blessing bestowed upon others and myself. Make holiness the function of all your relationships, and joy is what you'll receive.

STEP 3. PRAY AND MEDITATE

Through prayer we turn to spirit for help, and in meditation we receive spirit's guidance. These two tools are the basis of a spiritual practice. I encourage you to turn inward daily through prayer and meditation, practicing the lessons you have learned in this book. Remember to keep it simple. You don't have to figure anything out or push your prayers to be a certain way. Simply be willing to pray by turning your thoughts over to spirit. Then sit in meditation and listen. You'll be guided to everything you need in that moment. You will receive the Holy Instant. With prayer and meditation in your back pocket, you can release the ego, stop running, and enjoy stillness.

Remember that there is no need to pray for an outcome. Simply pray for inner peace. Anything you get won't solve your problem. The problem is always in our mind. The major shifts don't occur externally, they occur internally.

In addition, don't be afraid to pray with groups. There is a beautiful Power Posse (group) on HerFuture.com called Shared Prayer. Join me in this posse when you want a collective consciousness of women to pray for you or someone you love. If you're a man, join me in shared prayer on my Facebook fan page.

Finally, when it comes to prayer and meditation, let go of the rope. You don't need to manipulate your practice. Remember that your time spent in prayer and meditation is the time to relax and let your ~ing do her thing. As the *Course* says, *"You need not do anything."* Just invite spirit in, sit still, and receive guidance.

STEP 4. SERVE

I often found that when I'd think about all the problems in the world and all the opportunities to serve, I'd become overwhelmed. I felt as though the problems outweighed my power to serve—that's when apathy would set in. This was my ego's way of keeping me small and limiting my faith in miracles. As I've grown to be miracle-minded, I know that I don't serve alone. Spirit is my guide whenever my intentions are aligned with love. Rather than become overwhelmed with all the world's problems, I'd focus on solutions. Welcoming solutions and miracles allowed me to show up fully. I then got connected to particular causes I was inspired to serve, ranging from organizations that invite recovered addicts to speak at clinics, to women's rights organizations like Women for Women International and Girl Up. When I opened my heart to be of service to the world, I also attracted new opportunities to serve. My awareness of service guided me to serve more. My sense of inspiration strengthened my spiritual connection to the work, which opened my creative mind to execute innovative fund-raising ideas, powerful Internet awareness campaigns, and grassroots events. When you're passionate about the cause, spirit energy moves through you and empowers your service.

It is also important to remember that each moment and every thought is an opportunity to serve. Spirit-guided thoughts are of service to the world because they raise the energetic vibration within you and outside of you. Thinking with loving-kindness is a service. Open your heart to be of service to the world, and you'll be led to the perfect opportunities to share love.

STEP 5. TRUST THAT SPIRIT HAS YOUR BACK

Faith is everything. When you believe in love, you can relax knowing that *it's all good*. Remember that your willingness to invite spirit into your mind will strengthen your faith. The more we call on love, the stronger our love muscle will be.

I hope you use this book as a guide back to love. Remember that your work is never done. Each moment offers you an opportunity to deepen your spiritual connection and strengthen your miracle-mindedness. Keep it up, my friend. Keep it up.

Constant contact with spirit got me here. When it came time to conclude this book, I found myself putting it off. I wanted to savor the last chapter—take my time and allow the words to pour through me. And I did just that. I waited. I revisited all the chapters leading up to this point. Reflecting on the pages of this book, I was astounded to find that I didn't even realize what I'd created. There were stories and sentences that seemed as though they'd come from a higher source. I kept thinking, *I don't remember writing this.* This experience was a sure sign that I'd done good. I truly allowed spirit to enter into the process and guide me. Clearly I hadn't overthought the contents of the book, but rather allowed the work to flow creatively from my inside out. This book is an extension of my spirit and all the inner guidance that I choose to work with. By listening to this guidance, I've enjoyed every second of the writing process. I've healed more, learned more, and loved more. I've deepened my relationship with spirit throughout the collaborative effort to create this book for you.

Throughout my process of creating this work I've felt

a presence by my side. Often a rush of energy would pour through my hands, inspired ideas would come to me in the middle of the night, human guidance was always present, and new assignments led to authentic content. Each moment of this process has been guided, and I hope you've felt the presence of a power greater than me pour off each page. Each word, thought, and sentence is infused with spirit's love. Together let's say *Thank you*. We thank the infinite loving Universe and the beautiful spirit that flows through each of us. We thank spirit for your guidance, your inspiration, your lessons, and your support. We thank you for reminding us to have faith in love.

With endless love and gratitude, I send you off with a spiritual connection of your own understanding—a connection that will be yours to grow and share with the world, an everlasting companion on your miraculous journey inward. May you release your fear, have faith in spirit, expect miracles, and always listen to your inner guide.

Acknowledgments

There are many human angels who participated in the creation of this book. It is with tremendous gratitude that I acknowledge my literary agent, Michele Martin. I look forward to a lifetime of collaborations. A huge shout-out goes to Katie Karlson for your edits and divine spark. I thank Sam Bassett for your photos, Jenny Sansouci for your PA love, Haleh Nematzadeh for styling the shoot, and 5Pointz Graffiti Park for providing an awesome backdrop for our cover. Thank you to the Crown Publishing team at Random House: Tina Constable, Penny Simon, Jennifer Robbins, Meredith McGinnis, Annie Chagnot, and Tammy Blake for your enthusiasm and faith in *Spirit Junkie*. Trace Murphy, I thank you for being my editor and sharing my passion for *A Course in Miracles*.

Acknowledgments

I thank all the beautiful people who have offered me the most life-changing spiritual assignments. Thanks to my mom, dad, Mike, Harriet, Max, and all my grandparents for being my family unit this time around. We signed a sacred contract, and our love for one another is everlasting. I thank my beautiful holy love, Zach Rocklin: you are my greatest teacher and my dearest friend.

To my spiritual soul sisters who supported this book: Eliza Dushku, Latham Thomas, Elisa Hallerman, and all the women on HerFuture.com! I thank my teacher and friend Marianne Williamson. Your work inspired me to be the woman and teacher I am today. Thank you for setting me on my path. Finally, I thank John of God and all of the mediums at the Casa de Dom Inacio for teaching me to be an authentic Spirit Junkie.